It's That Easy!

A Proven Strategy for
the Individual Investor

It's That Easy!

A Proven Strategy for
the Individual Investor

Samuel Black Stewart

COPP CLARK LTD.

ISBN: 0-7730-5529-0

Although every effort has been made to ensure the accuracy and completeness of the information contained in this book, the author and publisher assume no responsibility for errors, inaccuracies, omissions or any inconsistency herein. The book is sold with the understanding that neither the author nor the publisher is engaged in rendering professional advice. Readers should use their own judgement and/or obtain professional legal, accounting and financial advice for specific applications to their individual situations.

Canadian Cataloguing in Publication Data
Stewart, Samuel Black, 1940-
    It's that easy! : a proven strategy for the individual investor
ISBN 0-7730-5529-0
1. Investments - Canada. 2. Portfolio management - Canada.
I. Title
HG5152.S74 1995   332.678   C95-932300-7

Copp Clark Ltd.
2775 Matheson Blvd. East
Mississauga, Ontario
L4W 4P7

Printed and bound in Canada

1 2 3 4 5   5529-0   99 98 97 96 95

Table of Contents

Chapter   *Page*

1. Money Is The Object   1
2. Setting Goals   7
3. Investment's Four Pillars   13
4. A Stock Market Primer   23
5. Borrowing To Invest   39
6. The Options Market   51
7. Writing Covered Calls   63
8. Using Put Options   77
9. Convertible Bonds   81
10. Technical Analysis   91
11. Record Keeping   103
12. Investment Management   109

Appendix 1. Stewart's 20 Investment Rules   123
Appendix 2. Glossary of Investment Terms   125

——————————————————— **Chapter 1**

Money Is The Object

"I have never had a financial problem."

This basic statement seems hard to believe and I certainly anticipate that I will have to offer some explanation. I have had personal problems and health problems, but there has never been a time during my life that I had a financial problem.

I grew up in rather sub-modest surroundings, but was never hungry. I worked at something for as far back as I can remember, and I saved every cent I could. There were some trying years. While working my way through university in the 1960s, money was very tight. I took all my classes in the morning, worked at part time jobs in the afternoons, then went back to the university until the library closed at midnight. I held a series of dreary jobs such as carrying brick for a housebuilder and cutting chickens in a meat market for $1 an hour. But, I paid my tuition, bought my books, and had just a bit left over for beer. I didn't have a car and couldn't afford to join a fraternity, but these were minor nuisances as I had no time for such things any way.

I was a commissioned officer in the regular U.S. Army for six years and started out receiving $220 a month as a second-lieutenant. It was enough. I married. Emily Jane and I started a family, and we had no particular financial concerns — the Army provided basic needs. I left the Army, became a school teacher starting at $6,000 a year (a cut in pay of

$4,000 a year) and it was adequate. After five years, I tried my hand at being a stockbroker (taking a cut in pay again) and did very badly. First of all, the stock market did nothing but go down, and I discovered that I am not a salesman. I saw myself as a "financial consultant" who just waited for people to bring bags of money through the door seeking wisdom. I was very wrong about that. There was also something inverted about my financial track record. Every time I changed jobs, I took a cut in pay, which is hardly the key to success. I returned to teaching and quickly re-established a modest standard of living.

Emily Jane and I have never had a fight about money. We disagree about some things, but we share the same values of thrift, saving and hard work. I have never had to say to her, "We can't afford it." In fairness, she has never suggested an unrealistic purchase, but notwithstanding that, I would not ever want to have to say, "I know the *whatsit* isn't working properly, but we can't afford to fix it or buy a new one." True financial independence is reached when the only things you cannot afford are the things you don't really want.

We've never budgeted. We just spend carefully, make things do, practise the art of do-it-yourself to the limit that is reasonable and safe, and never allocate money to this category or that. We don't save "for" things. We just save because we believe in saving. We have never borrowed to buy any personal items and were content to have used furniture and one semi-reliable car until we could afford new things. We did buy a house by taking out a mortgage, but only after renting for six years. We set aside money for our children's higher education, taking a chance on one of the first registered education funds. It paid an excellent return just as it promised.

Emily Jane is an absolute phenomenon on saving and cutting costs and this cannot be understated. The more you have to invest, the more you are going to make.

I have no formal training in finance. No degree in economics. But, applying what I learned during my stint as a stock broker, I developed a specific method and technique of stock market investing that is low-risk, high-return and successful. I say it is successful because when I was discharged from the Army in 1968, I had $5,000 in a savings account and my wife had about $10,000 in CDs. Today, we are financially independent, debt-free except for our stock margins accounts and a fully tax-deductible mortgage on our home. We compiled this record despite the fact that my wife did not work outside the home after marriage and I never earned more than $42,000 a year as a teacher. My purpose is to share my investment method with you.

I first became interested in investing about the time I was discharged from the Army. I had never invested in anything but a savings account and had no idea that alternative investment vehicles were available. I put a bit of money into a mutual fund and it did nothing for two years. Disappointed, I sold it and opened an account with a stock broker. My first purchase was 100 shares of Labatt's Breweries. I sold the stock three months later and made a profit of $200. Not much, and I sold it too quickly, but I was elated and rather "smitten" by the realization that I had not really done any work to make that money. My euphoria was premature. I made all the mistakes an over-eager investor ever makes. I trusted the stock-picking "experts" too much and commissions ate up much of my gains. I couldn't see market trouble brewing and took "baths" in 1974 and 1981. The bad years wiped out the good years and I was getting nowhere. I considered chucking the whole business, but decided to review everything I had done and see if there wasn't some fundamental opportunity that I was overlooking. I found it when I read about covered option writing and realized that I was taking untoward risks when I should be letting someone else do that. I began anew in 1982 and began to earn a 20%-30% return on our investments. In good years, I have exceeded that percentage by a wide margin.

■ Why This Book Is Different

I recently went into the local public library and scanned the section on investments and money management. What I found was more than disappointing. Years ago, I read the two standard handbooks of the time, Gerald Loeb's, *The Battle for Investment Survival* and Benjamin Graham's, *The*

Intelligent Investor. Frankly, I don't think a useful book has been written since. I found books in which the authors praised themselves highly, then spun such a confused web of "indicators" that no reader could possibly make use of them. There were biographies of the great mutual fund moguls and silly books in which the authors nattered endlessly about how compound interest really adds up: "Yessireee Bobby, if you invest big bucks every year for thirty years compounded at 15% a year, you'll have a whole bunch of money!" Thank you very much. But, no where do these authors state how or where they were able to get such high returns for so many years.

I am going to tell you WHAT to do, HOW to do it, and WHY it is going to bring you solid returns. I will keep everything as simple as possible and not try to snow you with complex terms and procedures designed to show how smart I am and how incompetent you are. You don't have to know everything. I don't know everything — just enough to make good profits. I don't understand the complex, myriad of clever, international transactions that allowed a New York bond trader to falsely claim he made millions in phantom profits or enabled a New York currency trader to lose $800 million in a single week in 1994. I have never bankrupted a formerly solid British bank. My intent (and my promise) as the title says, is to keep it simple and easy.

■ Who Should Read This Book

This is not for everyone. This is not about gimmicks or get-rich-quick schemes. I have never understood how anyone can seriously believe that he or she can buy apartment buildings with no money down. I try to avoid the word "rich" because that sounds contrived, and I will never suggest that you are going to reap the rewards of your efforts quickly. What my wife and I have accomplished took nearly two decades, but that is a very short time in anyone's life to acquire financial independence. I will never say the words "no risk" because there is no such investment. Every investment has a risk. I refer to my method as "low risk" because that has proven to be true.

A friend of mine recently asked if it would be worth his while to borrow $5,000 and begin investing using my method. I said no, because he has two strikes against him already. First, he is in his fifties and that is rather late to start an investment program with such a modest amount. Second, if he has to borrow the first $5,000, it is unlikely he is going to be able to continue to commit additional money to the program and it will never grow to anything worthwhile.

The reader I am directing this book towards is employed, has disposable income of $3,000–$5,000 or more a year to invest, is willing to study and pay attention to his or her investment program, is preferably at least fifteen years away from retirement and can afford to take some risks. This book is also directed towards an established investor with a good portfolio who is dissatisfied with the returns on his or her money and who wonders if there aren't viable alternatives without taking unacceptably high risks. I offer nothing to the person who saved $600 last year and wonders what miracles can be made of it. The answer is "none," because the brokerage fees alone would eat up so much of that sum that it would be fruitless. Buy a pig and a bottle of wine and throw a $600 party. I recently overheard two young men complaining of their lack of financial strength. One asked the other if he was presently employed, and the second man replied, "No, I realized I had saved about $1,000 so I took a month off. I think I earned it." I have no words of wisdom to help this individual. My philosophy is that when you save $1,000 you plunge back in and get another. And another. A recent survey found that 80% of the people in the United States said that it would be extremely difficult to raise $1,000 in an emergency. That is a shocking statement where the vast majority of people in North America consider themselves to be middle class.

My method involves the stock market, and to a lesser degree the bond market. If that thought frightens you, then you should read no further. The last thing in the world people should do is to enter into an investment that makes them nervous or causes them to lose sleep from worry. But, before you close the cover, keep in mind that there are dozens of independent studies showing that over the past forty years the stock market investor has fared consistently better than the person who pursued real estate, gold, art, or any other form of investment. Not every year, or in just any stock, but if you had purchased just 100 shares of Wal-Mart when Sam Walton first went public, you would have shares now worth $1.2 million. Shares of Coca Cola have doubled and split so many times, it's hard to chart the price movement.

I do not seek risk. I make a conscious effort to avoid it. Investors have been told repeatedly that risk and profit are at opposite poles; that you must sacrifice one for the other. This is not true. It is not necessary to take exceptional risks to reap large profits. I'm more than comfortable owning shares of General Electric, Disney, General Motors, or Coca Cola. I think you can be content with companies of that quality, too. I won't suggest buying anything but blue-chip quality companies, and I'm going to show you how to make much more money doing it. You can buy shares of solid corporations and double or triple the income shareholders normally receive from the same shares. It's that easy.

I add another caveat: this can be so much fun it's addictive. Ask anyone who has been a stock market investor for a number of years, and you'll get the same answer. Whether you have a good year, a bad year, or somewhere in the middle — the whole business is fun. Some people don't really care if they make money. They just like to call up their broker and talk, and maybe ask, "What's the market doing? What's everyone buying today?" They just want to be part of it. Some people liken the process to a giant game with millions of players. Making a profit is winning, beating the other players, beating the averages, beating the experts, and beating "the street." There is something compelling and fascinating about it all.

Chapter 2

Setting Goals

"If you know where you want to go, you will probably get there."

Time management consultants love to give their suffering clients an exercise everyone can learn to hate. I'm referring to the blank chart upon which you enscribe what you are going to do today, this week or this year. You enter things such as "Send a card to at least one friend" or something like that. Or, you fill up one of those "Things to Do Today" charts with really simple tasks, such as "breathe," so you have the thrill of crossing them off because you know you are going to do them anyway. I am being too harsh.

When I talk about setting goals, I'm referring to something much more specific and meaningful. It is very hard when talking to young people to get them to think seriously about something called "long-term goals." Questions such as "Where do you see yourself five years from now? Ten years? What will you be doing?" will usually bring a non-committal mumbling that implies that the very thought of being anywhere in ten years is in doubt. But, the same problem is true of many people in their forties and fifties. They may have some vague notion of a hoped-for pension somewhere down the road, but that's about the extent of their creative thinking.

I recently had a long discussion with a colleague who felt rather adrift financially. It is not my place or my interest ever to try to delve so deeply into another person's financial and personal life as to examine what he or she spends on food or recreation. However, I would note that when my wife and I read financial advice columns in magazines in which experts evaluate the problems of real or hypothetical couples, we are astonished at what they spend on food, clothing, and other items. We couldn't possibly spend that much money. For a number of years I moonlighted by preparing tax returns for people. It was not uncommon for a couple to have a combined income of $100,000 with no T5 tax forms (reporting interest or dividends). No bank accounts, no investments, a mediocre house and a broken-down car. Where does so much money go?

My colleague suffers from a very basic problem: He has no investment plan or strategy whatsoever. He simply buys whatever comes along. He has a small bit of vacant cottage property so far from any highway that it will be valuable in the year 2060. He owns a small trailer/camper that gets no use. He has invested in a time-share condo he never uses and that pays him nothing. He invested in a mutual fund at the top of the market and only recently broke even. If he accumulates a few bucks, he pays down his mortgage a bit. This is not a bad idea, but he has a very low interest mortgage and, at the same time, owes a bundle on his credit card which is costing him interest at 20%. I suggested he increase the mortgage and pay off the credit card balance, but he seems to think that is immoral or something. After all, the home is sacred but the credit card is just ... well ... just money. I don't think I helped this man much, but I tried to convey to him the importance of having a financial blueprint rather than just drifting and bumbling along.

■ Three Good Reasons

About ten years ago I read a rather good book entitled, *How To Be A Widow*. The author had written this book after the death of her husband and found that she was totally lost in trying to unravel the gordian knot of government benefits, insurance benefits, and what few assets she and her husband held. Her lawyer confused and upset her and the process of estate settlement dragged on forever. The most important message in the book was that she and her husband had never talked about money, investing, or what they wanted in their future. They just took life one day at a time, did a half-hearted effort at budgeting and kept important financial papers and receipts in a shoe box on top of the refrigerator. Many people invest the same way.

Gerry Tsai, the famous (or infamous) mutual fund cowboy of the 1960s, once said that three times a day he wrote down on a sheet of paper the "perfect portfolio" — the list of stocks he'd really like to own. Then he compared his perfect portfolio to the stocks he was actually holding and questioned why his actual list was different than his perfect portfolio. He would re-evaluate every stock he owned and justify to himself why he owned it. If he could not think of three good reasons to own a stock, he sold it. He created the "Three Good Reasons Rule."

If you have any background in bookkeeping or accounting, prepare a personal balance sheet. If you aren't acquainted with such a document, the steps are fairly basic. Without going into great detail, just write down on one side of the paper what you presently own (assets). Include house, cottage, personal belongings, bank accounts, vehicles, insurance, pension plans, stocks, and bonds. Total this column. On the opposite side, list your debts (liabilities). Include the balance of a mortgage, credit cards, car loan, bank loan, or any other obligation. Total this column. Subtract what you owe from what you own and this is your real worth. Another way to consider this calculation is to assume that you died. Your assets would be sold off, your liabilities would be paid, and what is left would be your worth.

Next, examine each and every asset and justify why you have it. Why did you buy it in the first place? What is it earning or paying you? Perhaps, as is typical of any vehicle, your car is just costing you money. If you have two vehicles, would it not be possible to get by with one? If you have $20,000 in government savings bonds, you have a secure investment, but one that is paying you a rather low rate of return. A large bank account isn't much good when the interest rate is 3%. Perhaps you own shares of a mutual fund that has lagged the market averages for years, but you keep hoping it will catch fire. If you cannot think of three good reasons why you own something, put a mark beside it for further evaluation and possible elimination.

Now, take another sheet and create an entirely different balance sheet. Date this one five years from today. List the assets you want to own. Don't be flippant about it — no yachts or airplanes. List the debts you realistically think you can handle. The list may not be radically different from the current one, but it should show an increase in assets and a decrease in liabilities.

It is because you have a plan — a blueprint — that you will not be distracted by quick profit ideas thrust in front of you. Ten years ago, I was offered a partnership in a new enterprise that involved preserving flowers by a unique chemical and pressure treatment. I declined the investment opportunity because it simply did not fit into the financial plan I had at the time. (The preserved flower business did very well for a number of years, but recently has floundered.)

■ Obtainable Objectives and Priorities

It is not possible or wise to do everything at once. If you establish ten objectives or goals, something is going to get lost in the process. For some people, one is sufficient. There is nothing wrong with one main objective such as reducing the outstanding balance on a credit card. Cost-cutting is an essential part of investing for the most obvious of reasons: if costs equal 100% of what you earn, there is nothing to invest.

Objectives and priorities have to be right for you, because when you achieve them there is a great sense of personal satisfaction. If married or living in a permanent relationship, you and your partner must agree on priorities because when you work together anything is possible. If you are at opposite poles, failure is absolutely guaranteed. One cannot be frugal while the other is a reckless, impulse buyer. For example, when a couple whom I'll call Tom and Susan established a workable, commendable five-year plan to work their way out of crushing debt, it lasted all of four months. Tom called Susan at her place of employment and told her that he had purchased a used snowmobile at an auction, had written a cheque that would bounce within two days, and did she have any good ideas about how to juggle the matter? Tom went off happily to ride his new toy while Susan spent an hour on the phone arranging emergency credit at 24% interest to cover the cheque. I cannot reprint what she said about Tom's mental faculties. However, to make matters worse, she decided that the only proper "revenge" was to make a purchase of her own. She signed an order for an expensive piece of new furniture, paying no money down, but agreeing to pay 18% interest the following year. So much for spousal teamwork. The "house divided against itself" proverb comes to mind.

■ Cost Cutting

I cannot and will not try to prepare a budget for anyone. I think budgeting is rather stupid. My observation is that most people spend far too much money and are equally convinced it is necessary. To those who might believe I was born with a silver spoon in my mouth or have never known tough times, you're wrong. Neither Emily Jane nor I had a pampered life. In our teens, we both held low-paying, dreadful jobs to earn money for our education. We worked and saved and made the best of whatever life tossed at us. When I returned from Vietnam in 1967, I was posted to Ft. Polk, Louisiana. There was no housing for dependents, and the only place we could find to live was in half of a truck-repair garage. We went in and out through the grease pit and the mechanics worked on trucks all night on the other side of the wall speaking in colourful terms to the rusted bolts. But, after a long separation, we were together again and that was what counted the most. What we learned and have demonstrated is that we could survive anything and make ends meet no matter what. We still have modest wants and pleasures, and that is not unusual. No matter what you think is your absolute, minimal living cost, you're wrong. It's below that and given a determined effort, it is far below that. Emily Jane has kept detailed records of her food purchases for more than a decade and can show that she has kept our family food costs at $2 per person per day while feeding three strapping males with lumberjack appetites.

You have to set your own priorities and make some hard choices. How important is your financial future compared to comforts now? Are there simple cost-cutting measures that you can put into effect immediately? Certainly, and the list is infinite. The easy ones should be obvious to anyone.

If you live in a house rather than an apartment, a vegetable garden is a must. You can save hundreds of dollars on food costs by growing it yourself. Stop eating in restaurants and pay no attention to the fraudulent claims that it costs the same as eating at home. The folks who prepare those studies include such nonsensical costs as the hourly rate you might have been paid while shopping for food and cooking it. When I read that 50% of meals are now eaten in restaurants, I wonder what has become of the basic skill of food preparation. Learn to cut hair yourself. We bought a Wahl professional barber kit for $15 in 1967 and Emily Jane cut our hair for more than 25 years. Figure out what we saved there!

Take a lesson from your parents and grandparents. They did nearly everything for themselves and practised re-cycling before it became a buzz word. I'll leave this topic because it is not the main thrust of my message to you. Where you get the money to invest is up to you, not me. I'll tell you what to do with it when you get it.

───────── Chapter 3
Investment's Four Pillars

"While it is prudent to consider the return ON your investment, it is also prudent to consider the return OF your investment."

I am, by nature and experience, a cautious person. I try to cover all bases and think things through before acting. I believe in the mental exercise called "worst possible scenario" before investing. This is a modification of Murphy's Law that involves considering everything that can go wrong. I then work through a "risk/reward ratio" argument that pits what can be gained against what can be lost.

No investor can be right all the time. If such a person existed, he or she would be rich beyond anyone's imagination. Those who boast of infallibility, and there are such claimants, are distorting the facts. They couch investment advice in vague terms and then claim after the fact to have been a visionary. Every investment newsletter writer in the world now claims to have seen the market selloff of 1987 before it happened. None of them did. I am content to be right three out of four times. The key is to not get killed when you are wrong.

However, caution and the need to preserve capital must not become so strong that the investor is paralyzed into inaction. It takes money to make money and if the investor refuses to make a commitment, nothing will be gained. At any given time, a perpetual pessimist can cite reasons why this is a bad time to invest. According to some notables who appear frequently on television, the sky is falling every day. But, before embarking on the most important part of your investment plan — the growth sector — it is necessary to take care of three others. A successful investment plan stands firmly upon four pillars: (1) insurance; (2) cash reserves; (3) pension and private retirement funds; and (4) growth.

■ Insurance

Insurance is a complex subject and not my personal area of expertise. The options available are so widespread as to be more than a bit confusing. And, insurance is expensive. However, I believe it is financially unwise to skimp too much on this essential pillar just to be able to pour more money into something else. Books such as *The Mortality Merchants* argued vigorously that life insurance is a hoax and mutual funds are nirvana. "Buy term — invest the difference" became the battle cry of mutual fund salesmen in the 1960s and 1970s. Some of those "go-go" mutual funds collapsed and went out of business. Indeed, some life insurance is over-priced and poorly crafted. I would avoid endowment policies and policies that try to emphasize savings too much over insurance. The rate of return on these policies is too low.

Young people tend to ignore disability insurance, believing they are invincible. They also find insurance expensive and postpone the day that they acquire adequate insurance protection. This is a common characteristic of people with other priorities.

I strongly recommend disability insurance and if it is offered as a group plan through an employer, it is a bargain not to be overlooked. When you add to this the obligatory auto insurance, house insurance, added health insurance and so on, it is quite clear where the expression "insurance poor" came from. I don't have a quick fix for this problem. Just shop around for good rates, and talk to your agent about ways to reduce insurance costs. If you have good locks and smoke detectors, you can get a small discount on your house insurance.

Consider a personal liability policy that will also cover auto accidents and you can reduce the amount you pay for car insurance.

■ Cash

Business and commerce students should be sharply aware of something called cash flow in a business. Briefly stated, **cash flow** is the net income plus depreciation and depletion allowances. It's all the allowable deductions not actually paid out. The importance of cash flow cannot be overstated. Many corporations have floundered, or nearly so, because of this basic problem. In its infancy, Mcdonald's Corporation came close to financial collapse on at least three occasions because the company could not pay its bills. It was opening more than 20 new restaurants a year, but had no cash to pay the salaries of its employees or to pay its suppliers. The company had land, buildings, and equipment, but no money. The company began paying head office employees with shares of the company. They could either sell them or keep them. In Canada, Power Corporation suffered the same problem. In its earlier years, the company was operating a rather broken-down bus line, but could not pay its drivers. The president hit on the idea of paying the drivers with bus tokens. When they asked what they were supposed to do with a bag of bus tokens, the president replied, "Sell them to the passengers."

The lesson here is that "Cash is King." Most investment counselors suggest that an investor should keep enough cash to pay for basic needs for six months. There are ample reasons for maintaining this margin of safety: (1) to pay for unexpected expenses and repairs; (2) to provide a cushion in case of job layoff; and (3) to act as a reserve to take advantage of a new investment opportunity.

I regard a bank account merely as an extension of my accounting system. I don't see it as an investment in itself. Money flows through the account as investments are bought and sold, bills paid, and revenue received. The balance wavers between $40,000 and $50,000 which is not a significant sum for us. It is also an essential part of our accounting system for tax purposes. It provides an accurate record and paper trail in case of an audit. The present rate of interest on a savings account is around 3%, which hardly qualifies as an investment.

It is important to have a good working relationship with a bank. Once the bank knows the nature and extent of your investment holdings, business activities and reliability, you can borrow for business and investment purposes. Your banker can also be your best business reference when you seek credit elsewhere.

■ Pension and Retirement Plans

About ten years ago, the United Auto Workers tried to persuade the "Big Three" auto companies that auto workers should toil for thirty years and then be retired. Their slogan of "Thirty and Out" was unsuccessful, but my own personal view is that thirty years is just about right — no one should work (at a job) past the age of 55. Life is too short to punch a time clock for longer than three decades. And — perhaps most important of all — too many people have placed all their hopes and dreams on life after retirement at 65, only to die at age 66. They retire and build their retirement homes, then die before ever living in them. They set aside their favourite hobbies for years, then never enjoy them. They collect travel brochures for years and never go. Even if they don't die, they fall ill and are unable to travel. If early retirement sounds good to you, then you must face up to some harsh realities. Unless, of course, you have a fabulous income.

The first is that you must invest 15%–20% of what you earn to reach the income security needed for early retirement. This will require a somewhat constricted life style. The second reality is that you might have to stay with the same employer. You cannot keep job-jumping because you will never acquire any pension benefits. The only alternative is to establish your own retirement fund. The third bit of cold water in the face is that you must start doing this in your twenties or early thirties. Keep in mind that in this rather difficult period of economic history, you may have nothing to say about when you retire. You may be given a "golden handshake" and turfed out the door with nothing except a severance pay cheque. Corporate loyalty, years of service, and a perfect attendance record mean nothing. My brother worked hard and faithfully for a large corporation that was taken over by another corporation. More than 1,200 employees, including my brother, were fired by a computer. So much for loyalty.

In addition to building up pension credits, invest as much as the law allows in a private retirement plan. In the U.S., Koegh Plans offer tax benefits. In Canada, the long-established Registered Retirement Savings Plan (RRSP) is of such extraordinary benefit it is hard to imagine anyone (employed, that is) who would be without one. The number of investment vehicles is unlimited, but I recommend bond funds that are sold by banks, trust companies, and mutual funds. These funds invest in government and corporate bonds. Although they are subject to some value changes as interest rates rise and fall, they are generally very secure and very stable. That is why I prefer them over stock funds, growth funds, or self-administered funds. When it comes time to retire, you want the money guaranteed to be there. You don't want to have to postpone your retirement because the stock market has taken a dive and your RRSP has dropped severely in value.

RRSPs are also a good investment because the contribution is tax-deductible and the interest earned is tax-deferred until you retire. If you can defer a tax for thirty years or so, that is as good as never paying it. Whether you retire early or at a later age such as 65, sock all you can into these plans because the last thing in the world anyone needs in the "golden years" is to worry about keeping the roof over his or her head or being a burden upon others.

■ Growth

Having taken care of your insurance requirements and pension plan, and holding back a reasonable amount of cash, there remains the most important pillar of your investment plan. You must make your capital grow. The cost-of-living marches relentlessly upwards, despite brief deflationary periods along the way. Governments layer ever-increasing taxes upon the citizenry, promising each time that this is the last increase. The promise lasts until the next government which declares that mismanagement by the previous administration will require new taxes.

Growth is really an oversimplified term to describe the accumulation of capital. This accumulation must occur at a rate faster than the cost-of-living and income tax rates or the investor is losing ground. The question is how to get that growth in a reasonably safe manner.

It does not hurt to have a basic understanding of economics, but even in the absence of such knowledge, there are some things that are self-evident or a result of everyday experience. The first is that the higher the return on the investment, the greater the risk. The lower the risk, the lower the return. If you put your money in a mattress, the risk is low, the return is nothing. Gold is pretty and durable, and when everything else collapses you can always buy something with gold. History has taught that lesson over and over again. Some investment writers recommend that you keep 5%-10% of your capital in gold in the event of a monetary collapse. I think that is too high. I recommend everyone have just enough gold to see you through six months to a year of financial turmoil. After that, if stability hasn't been restored, nothing really matters.

The second lesson is that what is hot today is terrible tomorrow. During the 1970s, real estate was hot. The newspapers regaled us with stories of the new tycoons who were "flipping" entire office buildings in a matter of hours. They bought buildings at 10 a.m. and sold them at 11 a.m. and supposedly made millions in paper profits. Some investors foolishly entered the game very late and paid absurd sums for real estate in Canada and the United States. The paper profits collapsed in the late 1980s and bankruptcies soared. In 1995, the Japanese owners of the Rockefeller Centre in New York City declared Chapter 11 bankruptcy. One basic truism had been forgotten: Real estate is a growth investment only during periods of high inflation. When the central banks raised interest rates sharply, all the real estate that had been purchased with borrowed money became so expensive no one wanted it. These investors had also assumed that rents on those buildings would continue to escalate sharply. They didn't, and all their cash flow forecasts were wrong. But, it was intriguing to read that U.S. banks had loaned Donald Trump 300% of the value of his real estate holdings. I wonder why they won't do that for me?

The mutual fund industry uses the word "growth" with reckless abandon. And, in fairness, some of them have produced consistent results. For the uninitiated, a **mutual fund** is a company that accepts money from individuals and then invests the money into stocks or bonds. By pooling large sums of money, the fund offers professional management and greater access to the market than an individual can obtain on his own. At least, that's the theory.

The downside is that there are now so many funds, trying to invest so much money, that the pressures upon fund managers are intense. In 1975, there were about 800 mutual funds in Canada and the U.S. Today, there are more than 4,000 funds and they are moving billions of dollars in and out of markets every day. A fund manager is under pressure to "produce and perform" at all times, lest he lose his investors to a competitor. The result is that funds have a shorter and shorter time horizon, dumping stocks the moment there is even a hint of bad corporate news. When interest rates fell sharply in the early 1990s, billions of dollars moved out of the CDs (certificates of deposit) in banks and treasury bills into mutual funds. The difficulty of investing all that money wisely made the problems worse. The result is that over the past three years, the majority of funds have not even matched the increase in the Standard and Poor's Industrial Average. The investor could have done as well by throwing a dart at a list of stocks. There is a herd instinct in the mutual fund industry. At the slightest hint of trouble, fund managers rush lemming-like to the cliff and throw millions of shares over the edge. It means that careful stock selection is always the first rule.

I generally support the concept of mutual funds and hold six different ones in my retirement plans. For some people this is a very proper and sensible investment tool. I find it rather incredible, however, when authors of investment books describe the stock market as a rigged game, and stock brokers as charlatans, but then praise mutual funds highly. *They are the same industry*! It makes no difference whether you buy stocks directly through a broker, or buy mutual funds which, in turn, buy stocks through a broker.

In the 1970s, when real estate was flying high, "smart money" chased condos and "dumb money" owned stocks. The stock market didn't fare very well, simply because too many people were selling stocks to chase real estate. High flyers also included baseball cards, art, and race horses. It was not a time of sound, prudent investment. One of the evils of inflation is that it makes sound investments appear dumb and bad investments appear smart, with the inevitable crash that must follow. Granted, if you knew exactly what the inflation rate would be and when interest rates were going to go up or down, you could make a fortune in the bond market, which is very sensitive to interest rate changes. But, you don't know precisely what is going to happen and neither does anyone else.

So, why stocks? Let's take General Electric as an example, since most people are familiar with that name. If you had purchased shares of GE in 1985, the average price that year was $15 a share. (This is allowing for stock splits after 1985.) In 1995, the same shares were worth $58 a share. That's an increase in value of $43 a share over ten years. As a percentage, that is a gain of 286% over ten years, or an average 28.6% a year. In addition, you would have collected dividends on your investment of $10.43 per share over those ten years. This increased your return to an average of 35.6% a year. I think this is a very acceptable return on your investment and I think you would feel very secure owning shares of General Electric. The company has been around since Thomas Edison met Methuselah and has raised its dividend every year for more than twenty years.

Having said that, suppose I told you that you can buy shares of General Electric, hold them, receive the dividends, and increase your overall return by another 15%–30% a year without accepting any added risk. In fact, you would reduce your risk. I'll show you how.

A sound investment, with a steady high rate of return. That's what growth means to me.

■ Real Estate

You may wonder why I did not include real estate and, in particular, home ownership, as an "investment." The reason is that I don't believe "shelter" is an investment any more than clothing is an investment. That is merely a selling slogan invented by real estate agents. Where you live is a personal matter. It doesn't matter if it's a shack or a mansion, it's just where you live. Or, as comedian George Carlin says, "It's where I keep all my stuff." Housing prices rise rapidly during periods of inflation, and people think they are profiting by this. They aren't. If you buy a house for $90,000, sell it five years later for $130,000 (a result of inflation) your "mythical profit" of $40,000 vanishes immediately because you still have to find a place to live. You are shocked to find that the next modest house you purchase costs $150,000. Are you better off? If you stay in the same house for the entire 30-year period of the mortgage, you will pay more than five times the initial cost of the house in interest and equity payments. That is, the $90,000 house will cost $450,000. Your hope is that with inflation the market value will have kept pace. Many people therefore mistakenly believe that this process of house change represents profit or sound investment. It doesn't, unless you eventually don't need a place to live at all, and we don't really want to think about that day too much. Just be thankful the government doesn't tax the mythical capital gain on the sale of your personal residence.

During periods of deflation, housing prices fall, and people are often distressed to sell below their purchase price. After all, they have become attuned to believe that this can never happen. Wrong, and many investors have taken the proverbial bath in real estate. On top of this, any house, condo, or other abode costs money to operate. It costs money in the form of mortgage interest, insurance, repairs, and utilities. It isn't an investment, it's where you live. It's where you keep your stuff. Enjoy it, but separate it from what you call your true investments.

This does not imply real estate is never a good investment. Some people do very well in real estate. They acquire good properties at low prices and either sell them at a profit or collect solid rent from them. After the Savings and Loan debacle in the United States, some investors were able to buy good real estate at fire sale prices. I congratulate them, but successful real estate investments are actually quite rare. When I see shopping malls standing half-empty and see yet more being built, I am glad I don't hold the mortgages on those buildings and I cannot see how anyone can profit from such a venture. Commercial real estate has been in the dumps for years and many companies are reducing their office space by two-thirds, requiring employees to share office space. I have attended real estate seminars, usually selling condos in Florida, in which the promoters used the most contrived financial forecasts possible. The mythical capital appreciation was going to be used to refloat the gargantuan mortgage at higher levels and the suggested result was that the investor would never have to invest any real money. Some even promised that the investor would receive payments from the mortgage company. If you believe that, you believe rocks grow. The promoters get wealthy selling these investments, not buying them for their own portfolio. Be especially leery of deals where you invest very small amounts (often less than 5%) to become a limited partner with unlimited liability. When these deals go sour, you are legally required to put up more money — much more.

Despite the upheaval in markets in 1994-1995 because of the U.S. Federal Reserve tightening interest rates to avert inflation, the hard evidence is that there isn't any inflation on the horizon. We are still in a deflationary period and temporary blips of inflation and higher interest rates mean nothing. In the absence of any real inflation, I just don't see real estate as the place to be. If after reading this book, you still believe real estate offers a better return on your money, by all means pursue it. To steal a line from Lee Iacocca, "If you find a better investment, buy it."

Chapter 4

A Stock Market Primer

"There is no stock market. There is a market of stocks."

The stock market is not particularly complex, but in recent years it has become somewhat prone to greater volatility. In the 1970s, if the New York Stock Exchange saw 40 million shares change hands in a single day, that was a major event. In the 1990s, many trading days involve more than 300 million shares.

There are numerous causes of this increased trading activity. The first is the advancement of communications technology that permits financial information to flow around the globe with amazing speed. The second is the inter-relationship of markets which never cease trading. Shares of U.S. companies are bought and sold in Japan or Europe while it is 2:00 a.m. in New York. The third is the development of computer trading and derivatives markets. Computer trading basically involves buying or selling "baskets" of stocks while entering the opposite trade (buy or sell) on the options on those same stocks. Computer trading was blamed for the severe market decline in 1987, but the stock exchanges have now effected rules to prevent computers from causing wild market fluctuations.

Another reason for the increased market activity is that there are many more public companies and entire new industries in which to invest. Although these conditions have made being in the stock market a somewhat rougher ride, the overall direction of share prices is not changed. It is just that the hills are higher and the valleys deeper. As the godfather of the mutual fund industry, Sir John Templeton, said in 1987 after the market's sharp drop: "Buy quality. Don't borrow money to buy stocks. You have nothing to fear." I agree with two of those three statements.

My discussion of the market will be limited to the things that you need to know. If you want to pursue your knowledge of the market, the stock exchanges publish numerous helpful books and booklets explaining each type of trading.

■ Some Basic Terms

The money you invest is the **principal**. By investing your principal, you hope to earn either interest, dividends, or capital gains. **Interest** is money paid for the loan of money. Money in a bank account earns interest. If you purchase a government or corporate bond it will earn interest at a specific, stated rate, expressed as a percentage.

Dividends are a share of the profits of a company. Dividends are not paid automatically, but only when the board of directors of the company votes to pay some of the profits to the shareholders. Some companies pay no dividends at all, believing that all the profits should be reinvested to make the company grow.

A **capital gain** occurs when an investment (or security) is sold for a price higher than the cost. If you buy 100 shares of Dynamic Corporation for $20 a share and sell them for $25 a share, you have a capital gain of $500. Conversely, a **capital loss** occurs if you sell the security for less than you paid for it. Most investors are in the stock market to make capital gains.

To buy the shares of a company, you must decide whether to purchase the **common shares** or the **preferred shares**. The preferred shares have a fixed dividend rate and are usually purchased by people, such as retirees, who need income. The vast majority of stock market investors buy and sell the common shares, which represent the true ownership of the company because common shareholders have the right to vote to elect company officers. In reality, this right to vote seldom means much because individuals rarely own enough shares to make the slightest difference. Some companies divided the common shares into A and B common shares, and usually only the A shares have voting rights. A pension fund might own 2 million common shares, which is obviously more significant than an individual's holding of 500 shares.

Yield is the rate of return upon your investment. To calculate the yield on shares, take the annual dividend rate multiplied by 100 and then divide by the current price quotation for the shares. For example, if the shares of Dynamic Corporation are trading at $50 per share, and the dividend is 80 cents per share, the yield is:

$$\$0.80/\$50.00 \times 100 = 1.6\%$$

When investors talk about "profit" on the sale of a stock, they are usually referring to the capital gain. To calculate capital gain as a percentage, subtract the cost from the selling price, then divide the difference by the cost x 100. For example, if you purchased 100 shares of Dynamic Corporation at $20 per share and sold them for $25 a share, you have a capital gain of $5 per share (excluding commissions paid to your broker). To calculate the percentage of gain, the formula is:

$$\$5/\$20 \times 100 = 25\%$$

The above illustration assumes that the calculation was made on an annualized basis. Most investors feel it is important to express capital gains this way because a gain made in six months cannot be compared equally to a gain made in a year. This is not necessarily significant, but to make such a calculation you have to express the numbers on a 12-month basis. For example, if the successful trade of Dynamic Corporation took place in just 6 months, then you would state that your gain on an annualized basis is 50%. A capital gain made in nine months would be converted to an annual figure by dividing by 9, then multiplying by 12. If a stock also pays a dividend, keep the two figures separate for tax purposes.

■ Opening An Account

A recent survey showed that 50% of the population don't know where to go to buy stocks. Shares of publicly-traded companies are listed on the major **stock exchanges** of the world, centred in New York, Toronto, London, Tokyo, and other major financial centres. Stock exchanges are privately-owned, they are not government agencies. They are, however, supervised by their own supervisory agencies and by government regulators who look for any evidence of illegal trading.

Stock brokers are licensed by the governments where they do business and also by the exchanges where they trade. Stock brokers sometimes use more impressive-sounding titles such as "account executives", but they ultimately remain stock brokers. The investment companies for whom the brokers work have **seats** on the major stock exchanges of the world. In addition, stocks of many companies can be purchased over-the-counter through computerized trading systems such as the NASDAQ. Once you have an account, your broker will know where to buy the securities you want. Stock brokers are listed in the yellow pages under "Stock and Bond Brokers" but most people obtain the name of a broker from a friend or colleague. Although firms accept "walk-in" new clients, the industry thrives on personal recommendations.

To open an account, you must complete an application form that will ask some very direct questions. Some people feel these questions go too far and invade privacy, but each and every one has been mandated by legislation in some form. For example, an applicant will be asked if he or she is married and where his or her spouse is employed. This is not meddling. The securities laws in all jurisdictions make it illegal for anyone to trade in the shares of his or her own company or of any company in which he or she is a director. The prohibition extends to spouses as well. Therefore, the company must know where an investor's spouse is employed.

For tax purposes, a social insurance number is also required. A broker needs to know something about your financial status and your goals. The industry has a golden rule: "Know your client." A retired person on a limited income has no business buying a "hot new computer stock" because his nephew recommended it. As you are going to be involved in covered options, you are going to receive a mix of income, growth, and security.

The broker obviously wants some money to open the account. At this time, make it abundantly clear that you are going to trade "covered options." This will require a **margin account**. With a margin account, you can borrow money from the broker. It is also important to know that you will not receive a **stock certificate** representing ownership of the share. The broker will hold your shares "long" in your account. You will receive monthly statements showing your financial position. A margin account is not a "right" and the brokerage firm will require a credit check just like any other creditor. Some firms are reluctant to open a margin account until a new investor has traded with the company for at least a year. Stock accounts are not government insured, but investment companies have private insurance.

■ How To Read Stock Quotations

A newspaper has a financial section that contains news stories that affect the business of the world. It also contains pages of stock, bond, and mutual fund statistics.

To read a stock quotation, you must know where the shares are traded. General Motors trades on numerous exchanges, but mostly on the New York Stock Exchange (NYSE). Company names are sometimes shown in shortened form such as GM. The quotation resembles the old "ticker tape" in that it uses short forms and symbols. A quotation might read as follows:

52-week High	Low	Stock	Div	High	Low	Close	Chg	Vol (100s)	Yield	P/E Ratio
65 3/8	41 5/8	GM	0.80	51 3/4	51 1/8	51 1/8	-1/2	18881	1.56	10.6

The quotation means that in the past 52 weeks, the highest price at which GM traded was $65.37 per share. The lowest price was $41.63 per share. The stock was paying a dividend of $.80 per share.

The highest price at which the stock traded this day was $51.75. The lowest price was $51.125. The last trade of the day was $51.375. The entry "Chg" means "change" from the previous day's close. Therefore, on the previous trading day, the last price for GM was $51.875. Volume in the hundreds means that 1,888,100 shares traded that day. The yield was 1.56%. The P/E (price-to-earnings) ratio was 10.6 to 1. The P/E ratio is discussed later in this chapter.

■ Why The Stock Market Goes Up and Down

Canadian economist and author, John Kenneth Galbraith, once joked, "One of the things that has always puzzled me about the stock market is why there should be a buyer for every seller."

There is, indeed, a buyer for every seller. The reason is that when millions of people, thousands of mutual funds, pension funds, and banks take part in a market, there will be buyers and sellers every minute of the day. The exchanges also have professional traders, also called **market makers**, who are required to enter the market and either buy or sell for their own accounts if there is a shortage on either side of the transaction. This does not answer the question as to why the price should change during the day or over a period of time. Why should General Motors trade at $65 at one point during the past year but could also be purchased for $42? Why does the market overall, as expressed by the "averages" go up and down? Cartoonist Gary Trudeau once made fun of this in his *Doonesbury* cartoon strip by showing a business news "analyst" explaining the market movements. The analyst said, "The stock market went down today. Our market experts say it was because more people wanted to sell stocks than wanted to buy them."

As pointless as that seems, it is correct. The price of anything rises or falls with demand. The trading on the floor of the exchange simply reflects that 'momentum." Let us suppose that Dynamic Corporation announced some very good business news. Investors would enter orders to buy shares. However, the investors who already own shares would be reluctant to sell them. They would hold them back. On the floor, brokers from many investment firms would "bid" for the shares. If these bids were not accepted, the traders would raise their bids higher and higher until investors owning shares would be willing to part with them. The psychology of buying and selling is the same in the stock market as any market.

Many things affect the markets, but there are three main forces to be aware of:

- *Corporate and industry news.* When a company announces its sales and profit figures, investors and stock analysts must quickly decide if the news is good or bad. The stock price will move according to that determination. If Dynamic Corporation announces that its sales went up 30% over the previous year, the shares will most likely rise in price.

- *Political events.* The political upheavals of the world always affect money. It is often said that stock markets "climb a wall of worry." If a war breaks out, a trade dispute erupts, a political leader resigns, or a government imposes a massive new tax on an industry, financial markets respond. In June 1995, when a trade war was averted between Japan and the United States, the market rose sharply.

- *Fiscal and monetary policies.* Financial markets are very vulnerable to interest rate changes, trade agreements, government tax policies, and budget deficits. Anything that will affect the ability of investors to continue to invest will either hurt or encourage the stock market.

■ How To Evaluate A Stock

There are many thousands of companies in which you can purchase shares. You cannot know much about all of them, or even a small number. You might become interested in a company because you like its products, saw a news item on television, or read a report published by your broker's firm. There are dozens of things that you might want to know about the company before investing, but some things are absolutely essential.

- **Revenue.** Japanese men do not greet each other with the expression, "Hello" or "Good morning" but with the question, "How's business?" You want to know the same thing about a company. Are sales increasing? Does the company have new products that will increase revenue? What are the positive things that are going to bring more money into its coffers?

- **Price to earnings ratio.** The earnings, or profit, of a company is the basic difference between revenue and expenses. A company's revenue might be rising, but if costs are rising even faster, then earnings go down. Most investors prefer to read the earnings per share rather than read numbers in the millions of dollars. In 1995, General Motors was expected to report earnings per share of $9.00. We can then construct a ratio of price to earnings per share, or the P/E ratio. The stock market price on May 26, 1995 was $45.00 per share. Therefore, the P/E ratio would be 45.00/9.00 = 5:1. What does this tell us? The basic interpretation is that the lower the P/E ratio, the better the stock price. The higher the P/E ratio, the less attractive the stock price. You cannot compare totally different companies, however. The auto stocks historically trade around seven or eight times earnings, while a technology stock might trade at twenty times earnings. But, if someone suggested a stock to you that had a P/E ratio of 100:1 you should avoid it. Something is out of kilter. For every dollar the company earns, you are paying $100 to buy shares. That is very expensive. The P/E ratio over a number of years is helpful in evaluating a company's prospects. Examine a ten-year history (from the company's annual report, a *Value Line* report, or a brokerage firm's study) of the company and note the high and low P/E ratio for each year. Suppose Dynamic Corporation has an average P/E ratio of 12:1. The highest it tends to reach is 18:1 and the lowest is 8:1. Suppose it is presently trading at 9:1, but the forecast is that earnings per share will rise sharply next year. As the earnings rise, the P/E ratio changes. Based on next year's earnings, the stock might be trading at just seven times earnings and is probably a good investment. Using our GM example again, some investment firms predict that General Motors will earn $11 a share in 1996 and $14 in 1997. This makes the P/E ration just 4.1:1 for 1996 and 3.2:1 for 1997. If these predictions are correct, the stock is trading at a very attractive multiple. The P/E ratio is only one tool of analysis, however. Nor is it possible to compare the ratio of a company in one industry to that in a totally different field. Technology stocks traditionally trade at very high P/E ratios, while automobile stocks seldom go above a ratio of 10/1. A P/E might be unusually high or low because of special circumstances. A low P/E doesn't mean a stock is a good buy if the company is having serious problems and next year's earnings will be sharply lower.

- *Solid balance sheet.* The balance sheet shows the company assets, liabilities, and equity (or capital). Some companies manage spectacular growth in revenue, but are doing it with borrowed money. In good years, this method of business operation can enhance the "bottom line" of the profit statement very nicely. However, in lean years, the effect works in reverse. As sales fall, but the lenders demand their interest and principal repaid, the profits of the company go through the basement like an elevator with a snapped cable.

- *Steady performance.* The annual report of a company will show financial figures for the previous ten years (if the company has been in business that long.) Look at all the key indicators, such as sales, earnings per share, the dividends paid, and the high and low prices for the stock each year. You can calculate, or estimate, the percentage of change each year. Consistency is a virtue in the stock market.

As an example lets look at some figures for General Electric:

General Electric				
	1985	1986	1987	1988	1989
Sales per share	$15.51	19.31	21.77	21.52	22.67
Earnings per share	$1.28	1.37	1.80	1.88	2.18
Dividends per share	$0.56	0.59	0.67	0.73	0.85
	1990	1991	1992	1993	1994
Sales per share	$24.63	24.93	22.18	22.15	23.10
Earnings per share	$2.43	2.55	2.51	3.03	3.35
Dividends per share	$0.96	1.04	1.16	1.31	1.48

Although GE did not increase its sales every year, the overall performance has been solid. Sales per share rose 36%, while earnings per share rose 181%, indicating strong cost-cutting measures and greater productivity. The dividend increase from $0.59 to $1.64 represents an increase of 181%. But, the past is the past. What of the future? Analysts who follow the company closely predict sales will continue to increase between 9% and 15% a year and that earnings will rise between 12% and 20% a year. Dividend increases are also very likely and by 1998 the company may be paying as much as $2.30 a share. That's a tremendous increase from the $0.59 paid in 1986. GE represents steady performance.

There are numerous other factors to be taken into consideration, and experienced stock market hands talk about cash flow, the market action, on-balance volume, and other things that affect the stock price. With time and more experience, you will add to your understanding of terms.

■ Market Timing

Is this a good *time* to invest? This question should receive the award for the question asked most frequently, and for which there is never a good answer. Market timing is a topic that dominates the television interviews of analysts and experts. There are newsletters that are devoted exclusively to the subject of not what to buy, but when. It is common in the financial markets for analysts to offer their forecasts for various markets, interest rates, exchange rates, and dozens of other important matters. It is so common that most investors assume it *must* be possible, considering how many people claim to be able to predict the future action of the markets and how many investors listen and act upon those predictions. Can you think of any other endeavour where so many people try to predict the future? To be successful, you must stop relying on forecasts. It is possible to find a person who will occasionally offer an educated guess that actually comes true. However, there is no person, theory, or committee that can consistently predict tops and bottoms in any market.

The ancient adage of "buy low, sell high" makes infinite sense, if you know when the market is low or high and if you know whether a stock is definitely going to rise or fall. You don't, and neither does anyone else. Yes, there are certain statistics that do warn of danger. For example, if the average P/E ratio of the 30 stocks that make up the Dow Jones Industrial Average reaches the highest level in eight years, it is a warning signal that stocks overall are getting expensive. If the dividend yield of all the stocks on the Standard and Poor's 500 is very low, this indicates that stock prices are relatively high.

There is something very rewarding about buying a stock at the lowest price it will ever be again. It suggests financial genius, but the reality is that it was probably luck and that it doesn't really mean a great deal. I have never been able to buy a stock at the low of the year. In fact, my observation is that I have a bit of the "King Minus Touch." As soon as I buy a stock, it seems that this is the signal thousands of people have been waiting for to sell it. In the long run, it makes no difference. Successful investment fund managers, such as Peter Lynch, Warren Buffet, and John Templeton, never concern themselves with trying to pick the top and bottom of either markets or specific stock prices. They consider the value and potential of the stock and, unless the price was very high, buy it. And, they hold on to it through good and bad markets as long as the company does what they fully expected it to do. Only if something goes wrong with their expectations do they change their position. An article published in the *Wall Street Journal* in 1994 concluded that despite the impressive results which Lynch and Templeton had achieved between 1974 and 1994, most of their gains had been made during just four of those years. If they had tried to jump in and out of the market, they would have missed most of the major bull markets.

This leads us to what is sometimes referred to as the competition between the fundamental investor and the technical investor. The **fundamental investor** is interested in the value of the company and its prospects. He or she is not concerned with the market action of the stock. The **technical investor** looks at the market action and the price movement of the stock and makes a decision to buy or sell based upon what the stock is actually doing. The technical investor doesn't even know what the company does, but tracks and plots the action, referring to such things as "market breadth" and "advance-decline line." For the person trying to jump in and out of the market, technical analysis takes on considerable importance. For the person who is in for the long haul, it is of very little significance. My strategy does not depend upon technical analysis, because it earns income during both rising and falling markets. The primary use that I make of technical analysis is trying to pick the stock price level where I will place orders. Technical analysis is discussed further in a later chapter. However, my basic admonition is clear: Don't try to time the market. It isn't necessary to be successful. Further, you can't do it and neither can anyone else despite claims to the contrary.

■ Dollar Cost Averaging

One of the most often touted techniques of investment is something called **dollar cost averaging**. This technique recommends against buying a large number of shares at one time. Rather, it suggests making regular purchases at regular intervals, such as once each calendar quarter. The so-called logic behind this technique is that because you cannot determine when a stock price is at its yearly high or low, you should spread purchases out and thereby acquire shares at various prices. As long as the overall direction of the stock is upward, dollar cost averaging seems to provide a "hedge" against paying the highest possible price for a stock. Mutual fund advocates also recommend dollar cost averaging. The problem is that dollar cost averaging is a dumb idea.

When I was a stock broker, I saw a client "dollar average" the purchase price of a stock from nearly $100 per share down to $4 per share. Each time he bought shares, he thought he had acquired a bargain because he paid less per share than the time before. Dollar cost averaging is one of those automatic mathematical systems, not unlike a Ponzi scheme, in which the perpetrators invent numbers that always make it appear that the "average" cost per share is consistently below the current price per share. It is equally easy to toss up figures showing that the investor's average cost will remain below the market price for a long time. If a stock or fund is falling on its face, you are not getting a bargain by purchasing more shares at ever-lower prices.

There are two things that work against dollar cost averaging. The first is that it greatly increases commissions by increasing the number of transactions. Each time you trade, there is a minimum commission that must be paid. One large transaction will cost you much less than several small transactions. The second problem with dollar cost averaging is that it tends to dull the senses which should be re-evaluating the price movement of the stock. There is a much more time-tested stock market axiom: "Average up, never down." Gerald Loeb (the Dean of Wall Street) was absolutely insistent upon this principle. If you purchase shares of Dynamic Corporation and it goes up, buy more. If it continues to rise, buy still more. If it declines or stops rising, stop making purchases and watch it closely. If you purchase shares of Dynamic Corporation and it goes down, cut your losses. Don't buy more shares until you are convinced that the decline is temporary or that it represents an aberration. Investors who have not lived through a real bear market don't realize how far shares can fall. After a 50% decline, they are inclined to say, "It can't go any lower than that." Wrong. Stocks can decline far deeper than one might think. It has nothing to do with value. It has to do with market psychology. Dollar cost averaging violates the rule against "throwing good money after bad."

■ When To Sell A Stock

Nearly every broker or analyst seems to know just what to buy and when. It is a rare breed that also knows when to sell. One of the reasons is that having made a '"commitment" to the stock, it is painful to admit you made a mistake or that you should bid adieu to a loyal friend. It is dangerous to become personally attached to a particular company. Don't fall in love with the stocks that have done well, and don't hate those that have performed badly.

Wall Street has a rule for nearly everything, and this is no exception. The rule is "Cut your losses; let your profits run." If you own four stocks, two or which have risen in price and two of which have fallen in price, the correct action is to sell the losers and buy more shares of the winners. However, most investors do the opposite. They sell the winners to "lock in their profits" and then keep the losers hoping for a miraculous recovery. Years later they are holding a basket full of losers and waiting for the resurrection that never happens. It is the triumph of hope over experience and common sense.

You should sell a stock when the expectations you had for it are not coming true. The sales are flat or falling. The earnings per share are weak because costs are rising, not being cut. If the stock price is falling, find out why. Don't sell it because of some temporary problem such as, "Investors are worried the Federal Reserve might raise interest rates" or "the Producer Price Index was higher than economists expected." When Borland, a computer software company, announced that the release of a major new product would be delayed several months, the stock fell 30%. This was hardly sufficient reason to dump the stock. The product was eventually released, made a great impression upon customers and the stock rebounded nicely. The market is filled with "panic sellers." Don't become one of them. Patience is obligatory. Sell a stock when it has truly been a disappointment, or you believe it has achieved all that you expected of it, and you are confident you can put the funds to work in a better investment.

You cannot take revenge on a stock or the market. When I hear someone say, "I am waiting until that crummy stock gets back to where I bought it and then I'm going to dump it!" I wonder if the speaker thinks he will hurt the stock's feelings. My usual response is that if the investor believes the stock will go up in price, then he or she should buy more. When it reaches the original price, rather than breaking even the investor will have a profit. Investors seldom do this, however, because they want to stay angry at the stock.

Avoid formulas and "mechanistic" methods of investing. For example, one writer advocated investing an additional ten percent of your cash position each time the market went down ten percent. As the market rose, you were to sell into the strength of the market. He was basing this entire method on his false notion that you would always be buying low and selling high. The fallacy was that the investor would have sold almost all his portfolio at the very beginning of a real bull market. You would also be buying into a bear market long before it had run its course. In the stock market, fads arise and fall with considerable frequency. In the late 1960s, two authors published a formula in which they argued that an investor would make money every single time if he bought shares of the stock and simultaneously sold warrants on the same stock. All warrants eventually become worthless, so the authors concluded that the gap between the two would become narrower each month, thereby guaranteeing a profit no matter which way the stock went. The theory broke down when it was quickly pointed out that very few good companies have issued warrants and that there is poor liquidity in that particular market. The so-called profit gap disappeared when the investor actually tried to buy back the warrants. Theory and reality are not the same thing.

You may have to sell a good stock just because the climate is wrong. Nothing upsets the market like political heat and politicians love to curry voter favour by crushing an industry. President Kennedy declared war on the steel industry, President Carter and Prime Minister Trudeau decided that the oil industry was the cause of all problems, and President Clinton won political points by attacking the drug industry. It is guaranteed that politicians never let facts get in the way. I held a large number of shares of Philip Morris for many years and reaped excellent gains. In 1994, I sold the stock for several reasons. It had engaged in a price war with other brands. It was under fire from Congress and the Food and Drug Administration over health concerns. The number of lawsuits against tobacco companies was growing weekly. I made a decision that the stock price would be adversely affected by these problems no matter how well the company was doing. I like the company very much, and the price has rebounded somewhat since I sold it, but I concluded that there are just so many negative factors that a stock can support at one time. The psychology was no longer positive and I think selling it was the proper thing to do. In 1995, after the Republican Party was in control of the U.S. Congress, I cautiously bought some shares of Philip Morris again. The political tension has lessened, and some of the lawsuits have collapsed. However, I don't think the company will ever get completely out from under the threat of legislative action or a successful civil suit.

Chapter 5

Borrowing To Invest

"No one ever made money except by using someone else's money."

The market debacle of 1987 brought running to television studios all over the world the best and the brightest to explain what had gone wrong. They were also quick to affirm that fundamentally, everything was fine — the market slide had been grossly exaggerated by computer trading and panic selling. On top of this, too many people had been speculating in the market with borrowed money. It was a good and healthy thing to "wring" them out of the market once in a while. That was little solace to the distraught speculators who thought the world was coming to an end. On the television program, *Wall Street Week*, Sir John Templeton solemnly declared that investors should never buy stock with borrowed money. Would I dare to disagree? Yes.

■ It Makes Sense To Borrow

I have invested with borrowed money for decades without problem. In fact, it is *absolutely essential* that you do the same. There is a fundamental reason for this: Unless you have one of the very best jobs in the world, you cannot earn enough money to ever have any money.

If that sounds harsh, it is. And, that is one of the most important truisms of investing. It is the lesson learned and taught by many of the successful investors in the world. Why not John Templeton you might ask? The primary reason is that Sir John is a very religious man who views borrowing as immoral. It defies the ancient prohibition against usury. That is his belief and no one should begrudge him his values. Having said that, it is also important to keep in mind that few people have had the acumen and grasp of world markets that Templeton has. We cannot hope to emulate his method of success, but we can achieve it in our own way.

You are confronted by two insurmountable obstacles that will deny you financial success: (1) your earning capacity is too low; and (2) you will not live long enough for the compounding effect to benefit you. As Duddy Kravitz explained, "If I really hustle, my kids will have it all." I will never suggest borrowing to such an extreme that you will be in danger of a calamity should the market turn down. Moderation in all things is a good rule, and it is a good rule in investing. During the October 1987 sharp market decline, one of the television news networks interviewed shell-shocked people on Wall Street. One man wailed, "I have lost all the money I had and all the money I will ever have." He added that he would never again invest in the stock market. If he was correct that he would never again have any money, the second detail had already been accomplished.

How did he lose so much money in what was only a severe market correction? (It wasn't a crash in any sense of the word.) The fact that such a sharp sell-off occurred in a single day was a disturbing fact, and subsequent studies confirmed that computerized selling programs had contributed to the slide. This has been corrected by new trading rules. It is obvious that this individual had become greatly over-extended in the amount of borrowed money he had invested. Once stock prices began to decline, his broker insisted that the man put up more cash which he did not have. This required his broker to sell his stock to obtain the necessary cash. The snowballing effect as the market went lower was that the broker was forced to sell this man's entire portfolio at bargain basement prices. Most likely, there wasn't enough money to even cover the man's indebtedness and he ended up still owing money to his broker. He had built an investment program with the stability of a house of cards, believing as some novices do that markets always go up, but never go down. Borrowing to invest requires discipline against the trap of greed. As leverage works for the investor, caution is often thrown to the winds with the inevitable bad result when markets decline. It is a lesson learned, and then forgotten, at least once in each generation. Success becomes excess as the lever becomes a sharp spear through the midriff.

This example of excessive borrowing is the exception, not the rule. Handled with care and caution, the assumption of a manageable level of debt in order to increase the return on investment does not represent a special hazard. Indeed, it represents the only real opportunity to break out of the tyranny of insufficient earning power and an inadequate life span. Let's suppose that Investor K, age 30, earns $50,000 a year. After all expenses have been paid, including the government's endless quest for tax revenue, he concludes that he can invest $5,000 a year. If he is able to obtain a regular return on his investment of 8% a year (a modest return, but by no means guaranteed) he will have $5,400 by the end of the first year. He will have $11,232 by the end of the second year and so on. Compound interest tables are regularly available that will spell out a rather unhappy fact of life: Investor K is not accumulating wealth fast enough to provide for a leisurely retirement, an early retirement, or even a secure one. He must invest more than $5,000 a year. As a minimum, he must invest $10,000 a year and he must earn more than 8% a year — every year — to end up with a meaningful sum. We have not even tried to guess what inflation might do to his investments. Assuming he retires at age 60, the cost of living may be so high that he has barely progressed at all.

Investor K might very well reply that he cannot possibly set aside $10,000 a year. Like many people, he might look for a second job and hope that some "moonlighting" will give him the added boost. Or, he (or she) might look for a job for his spouse, only to find that the after-tax return on her salary adds very little to their investment program. It is situations such as this that propels people to buy lottery tickets and hope that some rich relative will soon die.

Clearly, these are not viable solutions. The only meaningful solution is to borrow.

▓ Understanding Leverage

If you look at the balance sheet of any large corporation, you will find a section entitled Liabilities. In that section you will find notations of bonds and bank loans which the corporation owes to various creditors, including its own bondholders. Large corporations understand that they cannot operate and did not become large in the first place by just trying to make profits. They borrow money to obtain leverage. What's good for IBM is good for you.

The concept of **leverage** is very much like the device after which it is named — the lever. The lever allows the application of greater force upon an object than might otherwise be obtained. Everyone who has pried something with a screwdriver, iron bar, tire iron, or any other tool understands how it works. In the investment field, the lever is the use of "new money" which the company otherwise would not have. If the company can sell its products for a gross profit of 12%, and can borrow money from a bank at 8%, then it makes infinite sense to borrow the money and increase production. Let's use some hypothetical numbers to illustrate this.

Dynamic Corporation sells widgits. It costs $5 to make them and they sell them for $10. Using all its resources, the company can make 10,000 widgits a year. The profit picture looks like this:

Sales of 10,000 widgits	$100,000
Cost of manufacturing	$ 50,000
Gross profit	$ 50,000

If the company is able to borrow another $100,000 from a bank at 10% it can manufacture another 20,000 widgits with the money. The interest cost will be far less than the additional profit gained or at least the company hopes that this will be the case.

Sales of 30,000 widgits	$300,000
Cost of manufacturing	$150,000
Gross profit	$150,000
Less interest on loan	$ 10,000
Gross profit	$140,000

Using borrowed money, the company has almost tripled its profits. This is the effect of leverage. It should also be stressed that the interest on the borrowed money is tax deductible, so it would not really cost the company 10%. You are probably thinking ahead at this point and have correctly concluded that leverage works both ways. What if Dynamic Corporation borrows this money, manufactures more widgits, then experiences a slump in sales because widgits are no longer fashionable? What if sales drop so sharply that the company cannot even pay the interest on its loan? That, indeed, is the risk. The stock of companies with a heavy proportion of debt is leveraged to such a degree that the earnings of the company yo-yo up and down with interest rates and sales. During the good years, leverage works nicely. During the lean years, it becomes a huge stone around the company's neck. Many a corporate ship was smashed on the rocks of too much debt. A company can even be operating profitably before interest charges. However, after interest charges it is in the red. Sounds very much like our governments, doesn't it?

It is, of course, essential that the return on borrowed money be greater than the interest charged. It would be unprofitable to borrow money at 25% and try to turn a profit with it. It should not be particularly difficult to borrow money at 10% and do so.

When I first considered borrowing to invest, I was pleasantly surprised by a rather peculiar twist in interest rates. Short-term rates had come down to 7%. I borrowed money from a trust company at 7%, then invested it *with the same company* in a mortgage mutual fund earning 8%. I asked the investment officer, "You'll lend me money at 7%, the interest on the loan is tax-deductible, then invest the money for me at 8%?" He said that was indeed the case and I enjoyed this "free money" relationship for nearly two years before interest rates rose above 8%.

Let's create a hypothetical transaction for an individual investor. Investor K buys 1,000 shares of Dynamic Corporation at $10 a share. The shares go up to $15, so Investor K has a potential profit of $5,000. Let's suppose that he borrows money from his broker and buys 2,000 shares. The shares go up to $15, so he has a profit of $10,000 — twice as much. Even after paying interest on the borrowed money, Investor K is making much more money than he could with just his own money. Again, this is leverage at work. However, we must consider the opposite side. Suppose the shares go down to $5 a share. Investor K has lost twice as much money as he would have lost if he had not borrowed. The effect of leverage is to greatly exaggerate profits and losses. We need not dwell upon this point further.

■ Buying On Margin

Banks are in the business of lending money. So are brokerage firms. Borrowing money from a broker to buy additional shares of a security is called "buying on margin." Under present Canadian regulations, the broker may lend up to 70% of the cost of the security, requiring the investor to put up just 30%. It is neither necessary nor wise to borrow so much. Brokers won't lend to just anyone. Like any lender, they want to get their money back some day. So, the university student with zero collateral isn't going to wander into the broker's office and talk about a margin account. But, if you have regular employment, some savings or investments, and references, the chances are that a broker will offer a margin account. Keep in mind that not all stocks are marginable. Penny stocks which trade at very low prices cannot be purchased on margin because their true value is questionable. Also, the interest rate on a margin account varies just as bank interest rates vary.

The word **margin** means "the amount paid by the investor when he uses credit to buy a security, the balance being advanced by the broker against acceptable collateral." The collateral in most instances is the stock itself. That is, the broker will hold all stock certificates in the brokerage firm's office. It will not issue a stock certificate because the investor could then take the same certificate and pledge it for collateral elsewhere, leaving the broker with no security.

Interest must be paid on the amount borrowed, and this is usually assessed monthly. Let's work through a possible transaction.

Investor K buys 500 shares of Mystic Corporation at $54.25 per share. He pays a commission of $409.69 for the purchase, plus a tax levied by the Ontario Securities Commission of $0.35 (believe it or not) for a total cost of $27,535.04. He could put up the full amount. However, he decides to borrow $25,000 on his margin account and purchases 1,000 shares for a total cost of $59,270.34. The interest rate on the margin account is 10%. If the stock should move up sharply, Investor K will be making twice the capital gain as if he only owned 500 shares. He will receive the dividends on twice as much stock. The interest on the money borrowed is tax deductible (but in Canada not 100% deductible) so it doesn't really cost him the full 10%.

Of course, none of this makes any sense if Mystic Corporation flounders or the share price falls. To make any sense at all, Investor K has to achieve a return on his investment of at least 10% or more. Since the dividend on most stocks is less than 3%, this is not going to happen unless the price per share of the stock moves up.

If the price of Mystic Corporation rises, the broker will permit Investor K to buy more shares on borrowed money because the margin requirement of the account is calculated on the current price of the stock. Investor K may use his **paper profits** to buy more stock, but should do so with restraint. The paper profits will vanish if the stock price falls.

■ Margin Calls

Every day, the brokerage firm calculates the cash position of each margin account. The market value of the stocks is matched against the cash the investor has put up. The market value of the stock must remain at 70% or more of the value of the portfolio (and the initial cash investment must remain at 30%). If the market declines such that the value of the stocks is less than 70% of the value of the portfolio, the investor must put more cash into his account to bring it back to the proper relationship. The notification that more cash is required is called a **margin call** and the investor is said to be **under margin**. The rules of the exchange, and the account contract the investor signed, stipulate that the money must be paid in immediately. If the investor does not do so, the broker will begin selling stocks from the portfolio in order to raise cash. The decision as to what to sell first will be made by the broker. This is called **margin selling**.

As an example, let's assume that Investor K invested $30,000 in cash and borrowed another $70,000 from his broker to buy 1,000 shares of Giant Corporation at $100 per share. His initial position is as follows:

$100,000 value of stock	**$30,000 cash value in the account**
	$70,000 margin (the account debit)

Let's assume the shares of Giant Corporation fall to $95 per share. The $5,000 decline in the value of the stock is Investor Ks loss, not his broker's. The debit stays the same. The situation now is as follows:

$95,000 value of stock	**$25,000 cash value in the account**
	$70,000 margin (the account debit)

The client is now under-margined. How much? We calculate that 70% of $95,000 is $66,500. The debit that must be maintained is $70,000. Investor K is under-margined by $3,500 and must immediately pay into his account that much additional cash.

Margin calls should be avoided. In fact, an investor who receives a margin call has been trading "too close to the edge" and buying too much stock on borrowed money. No margin account should be managed in such a way that it cannot easily absorb the ordinary declines of the market or even a severe correction in the market. Although it is permissible to borrow up to 70% of the cost of a stock, I do not recommend exceeding 50%.

It is an old adage of the market: "Never answer a margin call" which means sell some stock rather than put up more money. My rule is: "Never get a margin call."

■ Pyramiding

During the 1920s, the stock market speculation that led to the eventual market crash was fueled almost entirely by horrific pyramiding of borrowed money. At the time, large "investment trusts" (the forerunner of mutual funds) were accepting small sums of money from millions of people to invest in their ill-named trusts. These trusts were able to buy stock with just 10% margin. For every 100 shares they could actually buy, the trusts bought another 900 on borrowed money. When the market went up, the leverage was wonderful. When the market fell, it was a killer. Everyone was willing to lend money, including manufacturing companies which became known as "country banks." The trusts were not satisfied with this leverage; they wanted more. The securities laws were rather lax at the time, so they were permitted to buy shares of each other. For example, Investment Trust B purchased stock on just 10% margin. Then Investment Trust C bought shares of Trust B on 10% margin. This was a leverage of 10x10 or 100 times. If just one of the shares actually owned by Trust B went up $1, then the value increase to Trust C was $100. To make the whole thing totally insane, Trust B then did a reverse buy and bought shares in Trust C. The leverage was now 1,000 times.

It was a time of wild, reckless optimism in which the trust salesmen actually told people that everyone was going to get so rich no one would ever have to work again. A thinking person might have asked who would grow the food, make the products, etc., if no one worked, but the question wasn't asked enough.

Buying on margin is leverage. Pyramiding takes it further. One form of pyramiding is to use the paper profits of your portfolio to buy more stock on margin. For each $1.00 the shares of a company go up, your broker will lend you another $0.70. A second form of pyramiding involves borrowing money from a second source to place into a margin account, which allows further borrowing on the margin account. For example, if Investor K has a portfolio of $100,000 and owes his broker $50,000, he has reached the limit of margin I would recommend. If Investor K could obtain another $50,000 and place it into his account, his broker would advance another $50,000 to match it.

What is this second source? The most likely prospect is a bank. The most obvious question is what collateral is there to give the bank if the broker is holder all stock certificates. A glib answer would be, "That's your problem." Well, I won't be flippant. I'll explain exactly what we did. We used our house as collateral.

If you're already mortgaged to the hilt, this is not useful to you. But, over the years, My wife and I paid down our various mortgages rather quickly. We did so most vigorously during periods of high interest rates. But, in 1991, mortgage rates had fallen so low there was no reason to continue doing this. Instead, it was time to increase the mortgage. However, we did it in a particular way so that the *interest on our mortgage would be tax deductible.*

We sold enough securities to raise the cash to pay the existing balance of our mortgage to zero. We then arranged a new mortgage, with a different lender, at a rate of 7.25% for four years. The monthly payments do not represent a problem for us. The collateral for the mortgage was, of course, the house. We invested the cash payout of the mortgage into our investment accounts. The interest we pay every month on this mortgage is now tax deductible because the proceeds of the payout *were used for investment purposes*. I want to emphasize this point. You must invest the mortgage proceeds. You cannot spend the money on personal items and deduct the mortgage interest. Under the current tax law, only interest paid on money borrowed to invest — called **carrying charges** — is tax deductible. This "new cash" injected into our investment account not only allowed us to buy more stock, but it also allowed us to borrow more from our broker and buy still more stock. The process can take on the appearance of an inverted pyramid with the paper profits piled on top of a much smaller initial investment. It is important not to let the pyramid become so top heavy that it will collapse.

There are two obvious dangers here. One is our old friend cash flow. We have to be able to make our monthly mortgage payments without difficulty. The second is the market itself. We have increased our leverage substantially by this arrangement. We obviously have to make more than 7.25% on our investments to justify this action. Experience has shown that we can always do this. There was only one year when our rate of return fell below 8%, but that was an aberration and the result of a fundamental error on my part. In a later chapter, I will talk about mistakes and how to avoid them.

I once thought that a person would be financially secure if he or she could just accumulate $200,000 in solid investments. I later changed that to $500,000. I rather suspect that $1 million is the true comfort margin. On a teacher's salary, saving as much as we could, we could never have reached that goal. Combining the stock market system I will describe, and greatly increasing the investment pool by borrowing, is the only way it can be accomplished. If you are intimidated by the idea of borrowing to invest, this is quite understandable. But, you should also be even more intimidated by the thought that no matter how hard you scrimp and save, it will never be enough. You cannot earn enough. You cannot live long enough. Compound interest is a silly little exercise in futility if you don't have enough money to start with and cannot add to it quickly enough. I have never felt threatened by borrowing to invest in high quality securities that pay a solid rate of return. I have felt threatened by the prospect of struggling hard all my life and still ending up with very little. Over twenty years ago, I took a look at the teacher's pension that I supposedly would be honoured to receive in the year 2001. From my perspective, it won't be enough to keep a canary alive. I resolved to make sure that I would never have to rely upon it as anything more than a minor part of my financial security. Recently, a retired teacher told me that he wished he had $500 to have his driveway paved. Although he had been working as a substitute teacher, he was still living day to day, hand to mouth. He worked thirty-five years to end up like that?!

It is remotely possible that the Canadian and and American governments will adopt a flat tax system. If this should happen, then borrowing to invest will be somewhat less attractive than at present, but this would not negate the overall compelling reason to do so.

Borrowing for any purpose has a risk, but I would rather take a risk and fail than never try at all.

Chapter 6

The Options Market

"I have never begrudged that fact that someone else made a profit, too."

The stock market has a companion, almost a twin brother. It is the options market. My method involves combining the two. Therefore, it is necessary to understand how the options market works.

Options are widely used in the business world. They have been in existence for centuries and are most commonly used in real estate transactions. The word "option" simply means a choice. You can either do something or not do it. An investor might be thinking about buying a parcel of land, but wants more time to make up his or her mind. Other people are also considering buying the land. The investor asks the seller for an option on the land. If the seller agrees, the investor pays the seller a fee in return for a written agreement not to sell the land to anyone else for a limited time period. The option also includes an agreed upon price should the investor buy the land. If the investor decides not to buy the land, the seller keeps the fee and is free to sell it to someone else.

A professional sports team might make a trade with another team under which it acquires a particular player and an "option" to pick up two more in the next draft lottery.

In the 1970s, the trading of listed stock options began in several U.S. and Canadian stock exchanges. Some of these later moved to their own facilities where nothing but options are traded today. The Chicago Board of Options Exchange is the largest of these exchanges.

It is possible to purchase options on just about anything. However, my method does not involve interest rates, currency, or commodities futures and I will not discuss how they operate. They are high risk and inappropriate for most individuals.

■ The Option Contract

The **stock option contract** is an agreement which grants the buyer of the contract the right to buy or sell (depending on the type of option) a certain quantity of stock, called the **underlying security**, at a stipulated exercise price (also called the **strike price**) for a stated period of time. For consideration of granting this option, the buyer pays the seller a **premium**. The option owner is not obligated to exercise his or her option but may do so if it is to the owner's advantage. If the option is not exercised by the expiry date, it becomes void.

There are two basic types of options: calls and puts.

■ The Call Option

A **call** option allows the holder (owner) the right to *buy* a specified quantity of an underlying security at a specified price within a set time period. One call represents 100 shares of stock. The price quoted is per share of stock. A call quoted at $3 means the seller will receive $300 for the sale of one call. Let's assume Investor K believes that the shares of Dynamic Corporation will go up in the near future because of good corporate developments. At the time, the shares of the company are trading at $24 per share. Investor K has the money to either buy 100 shares of stock or to buy ten calls. He has his broker enter this order:

> **Buy 10 calls Dynamic Corporation, expiry February 19 --, exercise price $25, at a premium of $2. Opening position.**

This order shows that Investor K won't pay more than $2 per share (or $2,000 in all), but most orders are simply entered as "market" orders which means to get the best, current price possible. Assuming the order is **filled**, what has Investor K acquired? He now holds an option on 1,000 shares of Dynamic Corporation. He has until the close of trading on the third Friday of February (options always expire at the end of trading on the third Friday of each month) to buy those shares (or any portion of them). If he decides to buy, he will pay $25 per share no matter what the market price is at the time. As this is the initial transaction, he is "opening" an option position. Because he is the option buyer, Investor K must pay the broker $2,000 ($2 premium x 1,000). Investor K will soon receive a computerized printout of his transaction which will state that he is now "long" ten calls on Dynamic Corporation. The notation will appear on his monthly statement as well.

The **long call** position means the owner of the call has the right to buy or take delivery of the underlying security at the exercise price within the set time period prior to expiration.

Investor K now hopes that his information is correct and that the price of Dynamic Corporation will go up. Let's assume it does, and prior to the third Friday in February the price is $34 per share. Investor K has the option (the right) to buy 1,000 shares of the stock at $25 per share. He could immediately sell them at $34 per share. As you can see, his profit on the ten calls was much greater than his profit would have been if he had purchased just 100 shares of stock. For an initial investment of $2,000, he has a capital gain of $9,000. This is our old friend leverage at work again.

Suppose, however, that Investor K was wrong in his hopes for Dynamic Corporation. Rather than rise, the shares fall to $20 per share. He now has the right to buy shares at $25 which are readily available on the market for just $20. He is obviously not going to do this and has lost his $2,000. He took something of a gamble and lost on this transaction. If he is wrong too often, he will soon be quite broke.

But, every contract requires two parties. If Investor K bought the call, someone must have sold it. Who was it? The answer is that Investor K doesn't know, doesn't care, and has no idea why that person did so. Although he has an option "contract" the reality is that the contract is actually with the option exchange and its clearing house, not with a specific individual. The person who sold these ten calls might be an individual investor or a professional trader. In any case, that person is said to be short ten calls.

The **short call** position means that the writer/seller of the call has the obligation to sell or deliver the underlying interest at the exercise price within a set period of time prior to expiration. The person who sold the calls received the $2,000 premium when the contract was made. This person will receive a computerized transaction record showing that he or she is "Short ten calls Dynamic Corporation exerciseable at $25, expiry February." This person has agreed to sell 1,000 shares of stock at $25 to whoever holds calls on those shares. To make certain that the writer/seller will actually do what was promised, his or her broker will hold the shares in the account.

Let's summarize what the two parties think will happen. The owner/buyer of the call believes that the price of the underlying security (Dynamic Corporation) will rise. In order to make the maximum profit, the buyer purchased calls on the stock which affords more leverage and greater profit if the shares go up. Prior to the expiration date, the buyer must make a decision to either buy the stock or not. (There is another choice, but I'll come to that later.) If the shares do not go up, the buyer has lost the premium paid.

The call writer/seller believes the price of Dynamic Corporation will remain below or close to $25 per share and that it will not be to the call owner's advantage to exercise his option. The writer believes that he will keep both his shares and the $2,000 premium paid to him for selling the calls. If this proves to be wrong, then the seller must sell his 1,000 shares for $25 per share even if the current market price is much higher.

■ The Put Option

A **put option** allows the owner/buyer of the put to sell or make delivery of the underlying interest at the exercise price within a set period of time prior to expiration. A put is very much the "mirror image" of the call. The call represents buying rights, but the put represents selling rights.

Let's assume that Investor K owns 500 shares of Dynamic Corporation. He is concerned that the stock action on the market looks rather weak, and the overall action of the market is troubling. His broker warns of a possible price decline. However, the stock pays a good dividend and Investor K thinks the long-term outlook is bright. The current price is $25.50. Should he sell the stock or keep it? If it drops sharply in price, he will kick himself because he didn't sell his shares. If he sells, and the stock goes up, he'll be annoyed that he disposed of a security that he really liked. What Investor K needs is a bit of "insurance." He tells his broker to enter the following order:

> **Buy 5 puts of Dynamic Corporation, expiration February 19 --, exercise price $25, at the market. Opening position.**

His broker determines from his computer that the puts are presently selling for $1.75 each, so Investor K must pay $875 ($1.75 x 500), plus commissions. What has he bought?

At any time between now and the third Friday in February, Investor K has a **long put** position and a guaranteed purchaser of his shares for $25 a share, no matter what the current market price. If the price drops sharply to $18, Investor K is fully protected because he locked in a price of $25.

Suppose that on the third Friday of February, the price of the stock is $28 a share. What becomes of the puts? As far as Investor K is concerned, they are of no value or importance. He is not going to sell his stock to someone else for $25 per share when the market price is $28 per share. He has lost his $875, but gained some peace of mind that he was protected if the stock had, indeed, dropped in price.

We must accordingly consider the person on the other side of the contract. The person who sold the five puts took on a **short put** position. He or she agreed to buy shares of Dynamic Corporation at $25 per share and for undertaking this obligation received the $875, less commissions. That person accepted an obligation to buy the underlying security. There are numerous reasons for a person to sell puts, but the primary reason is the income derived. Another reason is to establish a guaranteed buying price below the market.

Let's assume that Investor M is considering buying shares of Mythical Corporation, but feels the price is a bit high. It is presently trading at $64 a share. She concludes that if it dropped back somewhat, she would buy 500 shares. She then sells 5 puts exerciseable at $60 for which she receives a premium of $2.50 per share. This establishes her real price at less than $60 per share if the stock drops below $60 and she is required to buy the stock. If the stock stays where it is, or goes up, she will not be required to buy it, but will keep the $1,000 she received.

Assume the price of Mythical Corporation drops to $57 a share and Investor M is notified by the clearing house that she must complete the purchase as agreed. She buys the stock for $60 a share. Her adjusted cost is $60 minus $2.50 or $57.50. For the moment, Investor M is in a small deficit position, but keep in mind that her strategy was to buy the stock for fundamental reasons ONLY if she could buy it at a lower price. She has managed to do just that. Investor M could now just hold the stock and hope that it goes up. Or, she might immediately effect the other side of the equation and sell calls on her shares. The choices are quite varied.

■ Summarizing Options

The reasons for buying or selling options include the following:

Buying Calls

- *Leverage.* The call buyer can achieve maximum benefit from an increase in the market price of the underlying security. The price of a call is only a fraction of the price of the stock, but moves up almost dollar for dollar with the stock price.

- *Limited Risk*. The call buyer knows that the maximum possible loss is the premium paid for the calls.

- *Fix a Future Price*. The call buyer can predetermine the price of the stock the buyer wishes to purchase in the future. This may be advantageous if the buyer doesn't presently have the money to buy the stock but will have the money in the future.

- *Investing the Difference*. The call buyer may wish to invest the largest portion of his or her portfolio in fixed income vehicles (bonds) and invest a small percentage of the portfolio in calls in case the equity market rises.

Buying Puts

- *Insurance*. The put buyer expects a decline in the market price of a specific stock and buys a put as a form of insurance against that decline. The buyer locks in a price effective for the lifetime of the put option.

- *Market Hedge*. The put buyer who believes the overall stock market will undergo a correction can profit from that decline. As stock market prices move lower, the market value of puts increases.

Selling Calls

- *Insurance*. The investor who sells a call receives the premium and is partially protected against a market decline by the amount of this premium.

- *Additional Income*. The investor who sells a call immediately receives the premium, which represents additional income over and above any dividends that are paid on the stock.

Selling Puts

- *Additional Income*. The investor who sells a put receives the premium in return for agreeing to buy the underlying security if the option is exercised.

• *Lower Purchase Price.* The investor who sells a put may be able to purchase the underlying security at a lower price than if he or she had purchased it immediately on the market. This is true only if the price per share declines below the exercise price of the option. The investor not only can purchase the stock at a lower price, the price is further reduced by the amount of the premium received on the put.

◼ In The Money — Out Of The Money

Two terms are used to describe the stock price in comparison to the exercise price. Let's assume that the market price of Dynamic Corporation is $27 per share. Investor K buys a call exerciseable at $30 per share. This option is above the market price of the stock and is referred to as **out of the money**. If the price of the stock rises to $32 per share, the call which Investor K holds is now **in the money**.

An option may be in the money from the outset. Let's suppose that Investor K believes that at $27 per share, the price of his shares of Dynamic Corporation will fall, so he sells a call exerciseable at $25 per share. As this is below the current market price of the stock, it is in the money from the beginning.

The importance of being in or out of the money lies primarily in whether or not the option will be exercised. An option that is in the money is nearly always exercised.

◼ Option Price Movements

There are three things that affect the price of a put or call. They are: (1) the nature of the underlying security; (2) the exercise price; and (3) the time remaining until the option expires.

There is a fundamental difference between the price action of a "hot technology company" and a utility stock or telephone stock. The more volatile the price action of the stock on the stock market, the more volatile the options market that represents those securities. The price of an option can be as low as 5% on an annual basis or as high as

40% on a short-term basis. The more volatile the underlying security, the more the option market can push the price of the options higher. The objective is not to deal in those with the highest market prices, because the value of the underlying security may be very poor. On the other hand, if the option premiums of a particular underlying security are very low, there is little profit potential there.

The price of an option is partly reflective of the difference between the current market price of the stock and the exercise price. For example, if the shares of Dynamic Corporation are trading at $27, and the investor is looking at a call exerciseable at $30, the call might be worth $1.50 on the option market. If the investor directs his attention towards a call exerciseable at $35, then the market value might be just $0.25. The prospect of the stock moving from $27 per share to $30 per share within a short time period is a reasonable one. The likelihood of it moving to $35 per share is not very good and accordingly neither buyer nor seller is going to assign a great deal of value to that option.

Although the market price of an option moves in the same direction as the stock price, it does not necessarily move by exactly the same amount. The reason is that the option has already cost the buyer a premium that has to be recaptured before there is any profit. And, as the time on the option begins to run out, its price movement becomes less a factor of speculation on the market and more a factor of the intrinsic value it holds. If the gap between the stock price and the intrinsic option value becomes too great, computer trading quickly closes the gap as professional traders buy one security and sell the other. The basic theory, however, is that if the price of the stock goes up $2, then the price of the option will rise $2. This is not absolute, but is a rough guide. This is the effect of leverage.

Let's assume that on April 1 the shares of Giant Corporation are trading at $24 per share. November calls exerciseable at $25 are trading at $3 each. On October 1, the price of the stock has risen to $29 per share. Each $1 move in the stock is not necessarily matched by a $1 move in the call because of the initial premium. The price movement of the two securities would have changed as follows:

Date	Call Option	Stock
April 1	$300	$2,400
October 1	$500	$2,900
Profit	$200	$ 500
Profit %	67%	21%

The price of the stock went up $5 per share, but the price of the option rose only $2. This is because the buyer of the call paid $3 just to buy it. The **intrinsic value** of the call is now $4 ($29 - $25 = $4). Another way to think of intrinsic value is that it equals the amount the option is in the money. Yet, we see that the option is trading at $5, not $4. This is because it still has six weeks to run before expiry and the stock price may move higher yet. The closer we get to the expiry date, the more the option will trade equal to the amount it is in the money as the time element is no longer of any value.

The third factor, then, is time. The longer the option has to run, the more additional value investors will assign to it because there is still time for something positive to happen. A call exerciseable three months from now is not as valuable as a call exerciseable nine months from now.

◾ Option Repurchase

One of the most frequent reasons given by investors for not becoming involved in the option market is that they might be compelled to sell their shares and do not wish to do so. But, the investor has a choice. Having said previously that the buyer of a call option has the right to purchase shares of a stock at a fixed price at a future date, it is important to now consider an alternative to that stock purchase. The owner/buyer of the call can simply sell the call.

Options are traded on a market like any other security. If Investor K buys 100 shares of Dynamic Corporation and sells 100 shares of Dynamic Corporation, then his position is zero. Whether he has a capital gain or loss is not important at this moment. Let's assume that Investor K bought ten calls on Dynamic Corporation, and that the shares of the company have risen sharply on the market. Investor K could buy the 1,000 shares, which the calls represent, at a very advantageous price. However, if Investor K doesn't have the money or the margin to buy 1,000 shares, would his potential profit slip away? Not at all. He merely sells the 10 calls.

If he bought the calls for $3, and sold them for $7, he has a capital gain of $4,000. When Investor K bought the calls, his account showed that he was long 10 calls of Dynamic Corporation. When he sells the calls, his option account will record the sale of 10 calls as the closing transaction. His position is now zero.

If the shares of Dynamic Corporation did not go up, and the calls expired worthless, then Investor K's account will show the closing transaction as **expired calls** and Investor K will show for tax purposes a $3,000 capital loss. His position is now zero.

Taking the other side of the equation, let's assume that Investor M sold ten calls of Dynamic Corporation. The stock price has risen sharply and Investor M is advised by her broker that it is inevitable that she will be "called" and required to sell her shares of the company. If Investor M doesn't want to sell her shares, she does not have to do so. She has only to buy back the ten calls. Let's assume she sold the calls for $3, and buys them back for $7. She will obviously have a $4,000 capital loss. But, she still owns the shares and they have risen in value since she opened her position. Whether she should keep or sell the shares is a decision that she must make, but the point to stress is that she is not compelled to sell them. The investor must buy and sell exactly the same contract to have a zero position. If he buys 10 Mar 25 calls and later sells 10 June 25 calls he has two positions, not zero.

Puts are exactly the same as calls. The seller of a put has agreed to buy stock and the buyer of the put has the right to sell stock. There remains the choice of just doing the reverse transaction and zeroing out the position. The investor who has bought puts need only sell them, and the investor who sold puts may buy them back. There is no absolute requirement to either exercise a put option or to be exercised by someone else. Statistics from the clearing houses show that fewer than 3% of all options are ever exercised. There is no limit upon the number of option positions allowed, and the vast majority of investors close out their positions with offsetting transactions rather than exercising the options.

■ Rolling A Position

The right to buy back a short position or sell a long position, naturally extends into the right to establish a new position. For example, if Investor K sold his calls on Dynamic Corporation for $7, he is quite free to buy more calls with a later expiry date. Investor M, having bought back the calls she sold, may sell them again.

Closing out one position and establishing a new one is referred to as **rolling** the position. There are basically two things that are being re-established: the exercise price and the expiry date. For example, let's assume that Investor M sold ten calls on Dynamic Corporation exerciseable at $25 with an expiry of February. The stock price rose to $32 a share and would certainly be exercised if Investor M took no action. Investor M buys 10 calls February 25. This transaction cancels out the initial sale and the position is now zero. Investor M then sells 10 August calls exerciseable at $35. This establishes a new position at a later date and at a higher price. Investor M has rolled the option.

It is generally possible to buy or sell an option with an expiry date nine months away. However, recently some exchanges have started trading options with expiry dates several years away. They are called LEAPS (Long term Equity Anticipation Securities) and are available only on a select number of stocks. There is no distinct advantage to buying or selling LEAPS as the premiums are not as attractive as they are on the regular puts and calls.

Rolling an option position plays a pivotal role in my investment strategy, as I will discuss in the next chapter.

————————————— **Chapter 7**

Writing Covered Calls

"I don't just own stocks; I rent them to other people."

In the previous chapter, I discussed buying and selling calls. I didn't cover everything about the options market, but even what I did explain was more than you really need to know. You are going to do one type of transaction only. You are going to buy shares then sell calls.

You will recall that a call gives the owner/buyer the right to buy shares at a fixed price at a future date. For this right, the buyer pays a premium. The seller of the call receives the premium.

When I first began trading options, I did it wrong. I did it backwards. I bought calls. I paid the premiums and I then sat back and hoped that the shares would leap skyward and I would make huge profits because of all that leverage that was now working for me. It didn't happen. There were three common results that all worked against me: (1) the shares went down and I lost 100% of my money; (2) the shares sat still and I lost 100% of my money; or (3) the shares went up very little and I lost 100% of my money. The buyer of calls only makes money if the shares go up sharply and quickly. I never seemed to get that result.

It occurred to me that if I was losing all this money, someone was making money. Who was that someone? The answer was the person who was selling the calls. That person received handsome premiums, collected the dividends, and still owned the stock. The other person was the "landlord" of the stocks, and I was renting them. I decided I was on the wrong side of the transaction.

■ Covered Transactions

The term **covered position** in option parlance means that the person selling the call owns the shares that underlie the agreement. If the writer of the call does not own the underlying stock, the position is referred to as a **naked position**.

The primary objective in covered call writing is to obtain additional income in the form of the premiums. The premiums represent excellent value and a potential profit that far exceeds simple ownership of the stock. An additional objective is to acquire a bit of downside, short-term protection in the event of a decline in the underlying stock price. It can protect a profit against a short-term decline. If this sounds conservative, it is. This is why I said earlier that my system does not involve taking greater risk, it involves taking less risk. Having experienced more than one bear market, I am a cautious investor. I am often rankled by market commentators who say ridiculous things such as, "You should be very selective in the stocks you buy right now. I think investors should be cautious here." My retort is, "Is there ever a time you should *not* be selective? When is it a good time *not* to be cautious? Please let me know when I can throw reasoned selectivity to the wind and gamble recklessly."

■ A Basic Transaction

Let's work through a sample trade and then analyze what it involves. I will use round numbers for ease of calculation. Investor K owns 1,000 shares of Dynamic Corporation, trading around $32.50 per share. He instructs his broker to sell 10 calls, exerciseable at $35 per share, expiry date March (six months away). The market price for the calls is $2.50 per share. This is a covered position and the broker must hold the shares "long" in the account in order to guarantee future sale if the option is exercised. Any dividends paid by the company will go directly to the client's stock account.

During the next six months, the corporation pays two quarterly dividends of $0.50 per share each quarter. These dividends belong to Investor K as he still owns the stock. Let's calculate his return so far. Investor K has received dividends of $1.00 per share and a premium of $2.50 per share for a total of $3.50 per share in six months. That works out to a return of 10% in six months, or an annualized return of 20%. The investor who did not sell calls received only the dividends and has an annual investment return of just 6.1%.

Let's now assume that in March, the shares of Dynamic Corporation are trading at $34 per share. The person who bought the calls is not going to exercise them, so they will expire worthless. This leaves Investor K free to sell ten more covered calls, with an expiry date of perhaps September. He might prefer to go out as far as December and receive a higher premium. He will receive another dividend. And, he has a capital gain of another $1.50 per share since he first wrote the calls.

If things went this smoothly, and this predictably, Investor K could plan his retirement right now. With an annualized return of 20% or more on his shares of Dynamic Corporation, and with increased dividends over the years, covered option writing looks better than a fixed lottery. So, what can go wrong? Let's consider two other possibilities, although there are many more.

Possibility one is that the price of the stock goes up dramatically. Having sold calls at $35, Investor K might be dismayed to see the share price race through $50 per share with higher levels in sight. The person who bought the calls has made a whopping profit. Having paid $2.50 for the calls, they now have an intrinsic value of $15 each. Investor K of course wants to kick himself, and wishes he had never read this book, but this is the effect of greed working upon him. Let's consider what actually happened. Investor K made a profit. The buyer of the calls made a much bigger profit. There is no reason for anyone to be displeased. Investor K is

disgruntled that he did not get the maximum gain, but that's
water over the dam. The primary reason most investors will
not take part in covered call writing is that they cannot stand
the thought that someone else might make some money, too.
Money that they might have had. Greed is a powerful force.

Let's also consider the opposite possibility. Assume that
the shares of Dynamic Corporation drop to $28 per share.
The person who bought the calls has lost his premium of
$2,500. Investor K still owns the stock and his paper loss at
present is only $2 per share, not the $4.50 that the share
price has dropped. The reason is that the fall was cushioned
by the $2.50 premium. In fact, Investor K did not start
losing money until the share price went down below $30 per
share. If we compare this to another investor who did not sell
covered calls, that person has incurred the full $4.50 per
share decline.

So, the basic situation is this: In order to receive a higher
return on his investment, and also buy some downside
protection, the covered call writer is prepared to give up the
lion's share of price appreciation if it should happen very
quickly. It's the old tortoise and hare argument. Those who
play the market are running as fast as they can, always
dreaming of catching the gold ring — the next Xerox or IBM.
It never happens. They're never interested in singles or
doubles, they want only home runs. The covered call writer
takes fewer risks, plods along with a nice return of 20% a
year or more, and is more than content with that.

I prefer to let others take the risks and make more
money than 99% of the "hares" in the market.

■ Rolling The Position

It is costly and disruptive to buy and sell your underlying
securities too often. You have to constantly replace the stocks
in your portfolio if you are called frequently. This can be
avoided by rolling the option position. The process of rolling
involves changing the expiry date and possibly changing the
exercise price.

Using our example of a position in Dynamic Corporation,
let's assume that the stock is trading at $36 a share during

the first week of March. The calls which Investor K sold are now "in the money" and he will certainly be exercised and required to sell his shares if he takes no action. He has until the third Friday of March, but it is unwise to wait until the last day to roll a position. Investor K must enter two orders: (1) buy back the ten $35 calls; and (2) sell ten new calls at a new expiry date and a higher price. The intrinsic value of the $35 calls is $1 each, but they might trade a bit higher because there is still a small amount of time left. Let's guess that he is able to buy them back at $1.25 each. He then tells his broker to sell 10 September calls, exercise price $40. The current market price is $1.50. Investor K still owns his shares and now has another six months of running time before he must roll his position again. Any dividends paid in the next six months are his. His first transactions can now be evaluated:

Date	Transaction	Stock	Options
Sept	Initial Position	$32,500	
	Sold calls Mar 35		$2,500
March	Bought calls Mar 35		-$1,250
	Sold calls Sep 40		$1,500
	Stock value	$36,000	
Change		+$3,500	+$2,750

This is obviously a near-ideal trade. Investor K has kept his shares while they rose in market value by $3,500. At the same time, the call option trades provided an additional gain of $2,750. The pertinent question is, do all trades go so smoothly and with such good results? The answer is no. What is illustrated above is one of the very best scenarios. We see a gradually rising stock price along with good option premiums.

Many other scenarios can also be constructed. The most obvious one that comes to mind is where the price of Dynamic Corporation declines on the market, perhaps to $28 per share. The $35 call options would expire worthless and

Investor K might decide to write September $30 calls at $2 each for the next time period, with the following result:

Date	Transaction	Stock	Options
Sept	Initial Position	$32,500	
	Sold calls Mar 35		$2,500
March	Mar 35 calls expire		$0
	Sold calls Sep 30		$2,000
	Stock value	$28,000	
Change		-$4,500	+$4,500

Although the price of Dynamic Corporation dropped by $4.50 per share, Investor K is actually in a break-even position because the calls sold have provided some downside insurance. Investor K is hoping that the stock recovers and returns close to the $30 level where he has established his new call position. If the stock did return to $30, Investor K could buy back his present position at almost no cost and would now have a small profit. To summarize, the stock has actually declined in price, but Investor K has a profit because the premiums received on the calls was greater than the drop in share price.

Suppose the stock price continues to decline. Investor K does not have an "invincible position" any more than other shareholder. If Dynamic Corporation suffers a big drop in price, say to $18 per share, the covered option writer was only partially protected. Investor K could do some further repair by buying back the September 30 calls and selling calls at a lower level, such as $25. This would reduce his loss position even further.

On a more optimistic note, suppose the share price of Dynamic Corporation rises sharply, to $43 per share, higher and faster than Investor K expected. Investor K could let the shares be called away and be pleased with a quick profit. However, if Investor K wants to keep his shares, he must roll his position up, perhaps to $45:

Date	Transaction	Stock	Options
Sept	Initial Position	$32,500	
	Sold calls Mar 35		$2,500
March	Bought calls Mar 35		-$8,000
	Sold calls Sep 45		$4,000
	Stock value	$43,000	
Change		+$10,500	-$1,500

The result is that Investor K has lost money on his option trading. He was forced to buy back at $8 the calls he initially sold for $2.50. In the meantime, however, the value of his shares has increased $10,500, so he is still ahead $9,000. It is at this point that the investors who don't do covered option writing are quick to point out that if Investor K had just owned his shares and not written options, he would be further ahead. That is quite correct. There is a small flaw in that criticism, however. How did Investor K, or anyone else, know that the shares of Dynamic Corporation were going to suddenly shoot up nearly $11 per share? If someone had known this in advance, that person could get so rich so quickly that he or she would need no advice from anyone. The point is, that Investor K made a good profit in a rather cautious way, buying some insurance along the way. He did not get 100% of the gain, but did not take 100% of the risk, either. My experience has been that in a rising market, I normally take away 70% of a price increase. Someone else is making the other 30%. I don't begrudge someone else making some money, particularly when that person took more risk. I don't have to have it all, I just want to have more profits more often.

There are many different possible scenarios, and the investor would like to have the most gain with the least bother of having to constantly roll positions. I can make a substantial profit in any of these situations, ranked in order of preference.

- *A slowly rising stock price.* The absolute ideal situation is a stock price that is rising 8-12% a year in a steady, consistent pattern, year after year. The share price continues to appreciate, the premiums are good, and as long as calls are sold out of the money they nearly always expire before the stock price reaches the exercise price and it is not necessary to buy them back. Solid dividends add to the attraction. There are no ugly surprises and no sudden and violent changes in the stock price. A solid, rising dividend is an added plus, providing one of the reasons why the stock price is maintaining its upward trend.

- *A flat stock price.* The share price rises and falls slightly, but never makes a dramatic move up or down. The profits are diminished somewhat by the probability that investors will lose interest in the stock and the premium value will begin to decline. It is important that other investors hold out the belief that the stock is going to rise sharply in value or they will not pay much for the calls. If the stock becomes a "dog" (loser), no one is going to gamble on it. However, the income from such a security is steady and it is good to have a few "quiet" stocks in your portfolio that provide stability during market turbulence.

- *A gradually declining stock price.* It is possible to make money on a stock that is gradually slipping in price over a long period of time. Call options are sold, then expire worthless, and new calls are sold at ever lower prices. About 15 years ago, the shares of Tandy Corporation slid rather quietly from $32 to $18 over a two-year period. The stock then painfully clawed its way back to around $32 a share once more over the next year. For most people, this was now their break-even point and they might predictably sell it because investors so often say things such as, "If I ever break even on that stock ..." During this period, while others broke even, I had doubled my money. I had sold calls all the way down, and all the way back up. However, at this point, the TRS-80 personal computer became a hot item and the shares of Tandy shot quickly to $51, then $75! I sold the stock because I did not want to sell calls then buy them back at much higher prices. The stock had completely changed its character and was becoming too difficult to maintain a position.

Conversely, there are undesirable situations that reduce profit either because the underlying security is losing value or the security is behaving in such an erratic manner that the options have to be moved constantly.

- *A sharply rising stock price.* Although it is generally desirable to see the price of the underlying security rise, too sharp and sudden a rise means that call positions are no sooner placed, then they are deep in the money and the calls must be bought back at a higher price, or loss. If the stock price continues to escalate rapidly, the process repeats so often that the paper profit on the stock is being cancelled out by the losses on the calls. There is also the danger that the stock will then do a sharp reversal because it has become overpriced and will drop back far below the exercise price of the most recent call. I call this the "whiplash effect". As an example, shares of Caterpillar were rather quiet during the later part of 1993. In 1994, they suddenly shot up from $70 per share to $121 per share. (The stock later split 2-1). This rapid movement required that I buy back calls three times within a short time period, each time at a higher price. I was making a paper profit on the movement of the stock, but faring rather badly on the options. The last option was exerciseable at $125 per share. Profit-taking came into the market and the shares dropped to $105. My call at $125 was certainly safe from being exercised against me, but it had been sold after buying back the $110 call at a hefty penalty. The shares have since settled down into a calmer mode of behaviour.

- *A sharp declining stock price.* A gradual slide in the price of a stock is manageable and might be profitable if calls are rolled down. However, if the stock "falls out of bed" and drops like an elevator with a broken cable, covered options only provide partial protection. Although the existing calls will expire worthless, the next calls written will be far below the former price and will by no means recover the loss in the decline of the stock price. The obvious objective is to avoid stocks that are too volatile. For this reason, I generally do not purchase computer or technology stocks. The slightest hint of bad corporate news can cause the stock price to fall 30%–40% in a single day.

• *A boring stock.* Utility shares and stocks with high dividend payouts are sometimes called "widows and orphans" stocks. They are unexciting and even though options are available for them, the premiums are so small as to be almost non-existent. There is simply no money to be made here. The only possible exception to the rule is a convertible-preferred stock. The shares have a high dividend yield, and it is permissible to sell calls against them based on the possible conversion to the common shares. For example, if the convertible preferred shares are convertible into common shares on a basis of 3 to 1, then for each 100 shares of convertible preferred the investor owns, he is permitted to sell three calls rather than just one call. This exception sounds more interesting than it really is, because good quality preferred stock is becoming a rarity in the market.

■ Options In A Bear Market

If an investor knew with certainty that the stock market would become a major bear market, the best course of action would be to sell all stocks. But, bear markets never announce themselves with horns and gongs. They just slide under the door. However, if the market action of a stock appears weak, or there has been a sharp run-up in price which appears to have run its course, rather than sell the stock, the positioning of the calls can be changed. In the previous examples, I suggested placing the exercise price above the stock price in an out of the money position. During a declining market, it is better to do the opposite, which is to place the exercise price below the stock price. Should the stock price decline continue, then the calls can be rolled down. Because a call is in the money, it brings a high premium because it has not only a time value but an intrinsic value, too.

For example, if Investor K holds 1,000 shares of Dynamic Corporation, with a current price of $32.50, and believes the stock will undergo a price drop, he sells 10 March calls at $30, which is $2 in the money. A reasonable estimate of the premium would be $5.50. If he is right, and the stock drops to $27, then Investor K was well-protected against the decline by this defensive action of selling an in the money call. After these calls expire, he writes new calls in the money exerciseable at $25 per share. The premium is $6 per share.

I decided to give the stock a final value of just $25 per share because that's the price at which Investor K agreed to sell it. For valuation purposes, that is all it is worth. In psychological terms, this will not create a very happy situation. An investor always likes a rising market and is more at home writing options in a rising market. However, stock prices go up *and down*, and option strategies can deal with either situation. The result would appear as follows:

Date	Transaction	Stock	Options
Sept	Initial Position	$32,500	
	Sold calls Mar 30		$5,500
March	Mar 30 calls expire		$0
	Sold calls Sep 25		$6,000
	Stock value	$25,000	
Change		-$7,500	+$11,500

■ Double Dipping

Normally, the relationship of call to stock is one to one. That is, one call represents 100 shares. In a few situations, it may be quite reasonable to sell two calls for 100 shares. The situation I refer to is one where the exercise price is now so high that it represents no real value. It could be bought back, but this will incur a commission that could be avoided.

For example, let's suppose that Investor M sold calls on Mythical Corporation exerciseable at $80 per share. The stock market, and the shares of Mythical Corporation, drop sharply. The stock price settles down at $67 a share and for several weeks trades in a narrow range. The option has another three months to go before it expires, and Investor M is convinced that there is absolutely no likelihood that anything is going to happen to push the stock price to $80 within that time period. She could wait until the call expires and write a new one, perhaps at $70. But, in the meantime, no new revenue will be received. Investor M could take a chance and sell the call at $70 immediately. She now has two calls against just 100 shares of stock. The second call is naked. Her broker will require some more margin for this exposed position. If, for some reason, the stock price vaulted over $80, Investor M will have to buy another 100 shares to meet her obligation. Or, she will have to buy back one of the calls. This is a risk, but it is not a great one. It affords extra income as the same 100 shares are made to do double duty. Don't over-use this tactic, however. There is still the risk of some unexpected event, such as a stock takeover, that would cause the shares to jump.

■ Splitting Option Levels

The decision about where to establish an exercise price is often a difficult one. During a rising market, calls are generally sold at the next highest level. That is, if the stock is trading around $32 per share, the logical choice would be an exercise price of $35. However, if the market has become rather choppy and seems directionless, the investor is tempted to sell in-the-money calls for added security. The same difficulty of choice faces an investor with a large capital gain in a stock. The investor feels a strong urge to sell the stock, but also suspects the price will go higher and he will regret having sold it too soon. My advice has always been to sell half, keep half. That way, the investor is reassured that he can't be completely wrong no matter what happens.

The placing of option levels can be done the same way. Let's assume that Investor K holds 1,000 shares of Dynamic Corporation now at $32 per share. The stock has been bouncing between $28 and $37 over the past nine months. Investor K feels the stock is either going to break out on the upside or downside, but doesn't know which. In this situation, the best choice is to sell 5 calls exerciseable at $35 and 5 calls exerciseable at $30. He will receive premiums of around $7 total per share, a very good return and insurance against a sharp decline in the stock. If the stock goes higher, Investor K will have to decide if he wants to buy back the $30 calls at a rather stiff price or just let half of his stock be called away. The principle that I am stressing is that when uncertain whether to take Choice A or Choice B, split your position and take some of both. It's not unlike having to choose between two tasty desserts. Take some of each. One of them will be better than the other, but both are still good.

■ Calm In A Storm

One of the purposes of option writing is to reduce the anxiety you might feel about the market. It is therefore important to avoid getting into the same problem with the option market. Some option traders begin to fret about their option position as much as they did about the stock position. This is a long-term, gradualist system. It is neither necessary nor wise to tinker with their option position.

Let's assume that Investor K has sold 10 calls on his Dynamic Corporation exerciseable at $35. The calls expire in nine months. Within a month, good corporate news propels the stock price to $37. Investor K, seeing that his present position is in the money, buys back the $35 calls and sells the $40 calls even though the calls had eight months yet to run. The stock rises to $38, then slides back to $34. Investor K now sees his $40 calls as being very far out of the money and buys them back to re-establish his $35 position. The stock rises to $36. This "whip sawing" effect will prove to be very expensive when all the commissions are calculated.

My example might be exaggerated but it shows that Investor K is chasing the stock and paying commissions every time he changes his call position. Once a position is established, sit back and relax and don't try to "fine tune" it. Unless something very dramatic happens, leave the calls alone until they are near the expiration date.

There is only one factor that might require changing an option position earlier. If the stock pays a hefty dividend and the call is in the money, you will have the stock called away by someone who wants the dividend. Pay attention to dividend dates and roll your position before you are called. It is a prudent idea to put the dividend dates on a computer calendar of some sort so there is no chance of overlooking this important date.

Although I said that options should not be moved until close to the expiry date, I make an exception if the stock moved up sharply immediately after establishing the position. If the stock has suddenly moved to a new trading zone, rolling the option immediately usually can be done with only a small penalty.

The tendency to exercise options far in advance comes primarily from foreign investors where tax laws allow special treatment for writing options, then exercising them just prior to the payment of a dividend. There is no sure way to guard against this happening. If the stock is called away, however, the investor can at least be comforted by the fact that he or she made a good profit.

Chapter 8

Using Put Options

"You cannot always buy low and sell high, but you can buy a little lower and sell a little higher."

The put option has some important uses, although it represents only a fraction of my trading. For some reason, puts are harder to understand than calls and they are not used as frequently even by experienced investors.

The buyer/writer of the put option acquires the right to sell his stock at a set price. For this right he pays a premium to the seller of the put. I don't buy puts, but I do sell them for two reason: to buy more stock at a lower price and for some added income.

■ Using Puts To Buy More Stock

When I acquire a new position in a stock not previously owned, I establish a mental target of how many shares I anticipate buying within a time period, normally a year. I purchase half the number of shares immediately and sell covered calls against them. At this point, I might just watch the price movement of the stock and perhaps nibble away and acquire more shares.

I prefer to sell some in-the-money puts. If the stock price rises, then I will keep the premiums on the puts and perhaps sell some more. If the stock price falls, then I will acquire more shares at a lower price. At first glance, this might sound contrary to my earlier declaration against averaging down, but this is a different situation. I have already determined that I am prepared to buy the shares at the price where the first purchase was made. The opportunity to buy them within a short period of time at a slightly lower price is not a new purchase, but the completion of the purchase I have already decided upon.

Once the puts are exercised and I have acquired more shares, I immediately sell calls against these additional shares. When the premium received for the puts is combined with the premium received for the calls, the average cost per share is very advantageous and far below the market price.

Let's assume that Investor K purchases 500 shares of Dynamic Corporation at $32 per share and sells the March $35 calls. He might receive a premium of $3 per share. He also sells 5 puts on Dynamic Corporation exerciseable at $30 for which he receives a premium of $2 each. By March, the stock price of Dynamic Corporation has dropped to $29 and Investor K is required to purchase an additional 500 shares at $30. He immediately sells 10 calls on all his shares, exerciseable at $30 and receives a premium of $3 each. His average cost per share of the 1,000 shares is calculated as follows:

Date	Transaction	Stock	Options
Sept	Bought 500 shares	$16,000	
	Sold 5 calls Mar 35		$1,500
	Sold 5 puts Mar 30		$1,000
March	Bought 500 shares	$15,000	
	Sold 10 calls Sept 30		$3,000
Total		+$31,000	+$5,500
Average cost per share (stock − options) = $25.50			

Investor K has acquired the 1,000 shares of Dynamic Corporation at a more advantageous price than if he had just bought them outright at $32 per share. This example presumes, of course, that the drop in stock price is a normal fluctuation of the market. Keep in mind that the obligation upon the seller of a put option is unlimited. If the stock dropped to $1 a share, Investor K would have to purchase the shares at $30. Therefore, it is unwise to over-use this technique.

■ Using Puts For Added Income

If the shares of a stock give evidence of a constant, strong upward movement, there is an opportunity to earn additional revenue by selling puts.

For example, during the period from the end of 1991 to the middle of 1994, the shares of Caterpillar Corporation went through a long, relentless upward drive from $70 per share to a peak of $121 per share. The company had revamped its entire manufacturing process, weathered a difficult strike and was reaping the benefits of its new productivity drive. By selling in-the-money puts every six months, all of which expired worthless, I earned considerable additional income on top of the call premiums received.

Stock charts are helpful for this process. In a later chapter, I will discuss basic technical analysis. A chart can point out the price at which a stock is likely to find "support" if it declines. Selling puts at that level reduces the risk factor considerably.

This practice should be kept at a modest level. Keep in mind that these are naked positions that require the purchase of additional shares in the event the stock price suddenly drops. Selling puts represents only about 10% of my trading and I never take on a larger position than cash reserves would permit me to buy the shares.

■ Using Puts To Cover A Short Position

A professional trader who believes a stock is grossly over-priced tries to make a profit by selling short the shares. This process involves borrowing shares of the stock from a broker and selling them. The investor who does this has sold shares he or she does not own, which creates a "short position" in his or her account. This is a rather dangerous position, because if the stock continues to rise, the short position loses money because eventually the investor has to buy back the shares and return them to the owner (in reality to the broker.) In order to avoid the possibility of "taking a bath" the investor who sells a stock short also buys a few puts on the same stock. This "insurance" costs very little, but it means that if the stock continues the rise, the value of the puts will increase dramatically, thus avoiding the bath.

Short selling is very risky and I do not recommend it. We will not be using puts in this fashion.

Chapter 9

Convertible Bonds

"It doesn't get any better than this."

If at this point, you are not convinced that participation in the stock market is how you want to invest, there is an even more conservative way to make outstanding profits. It involves something called the convertible bond or convertible debenture.

Before you say, "Oh, that's old hat," I want to emphasize that you are not going to just buy convertible debentures and hope that interest rates fall or that the corporation prospers enough to push the value of these debentures higher. What you are going to do — *and I have not seen this explained in any other investment guide* — is buy convertible debentures and sell a large number of covered calls against them. Few people, even seasoned investors, are aware that this is permissible, and it necessarily follows that few realize how very profitable this investment method can be. And, it is even less risky than buying stock and selling calls. If this investment technique doesn't appeal to you, I doubt anything will.

■ Bond Structure

A **convertible bond** is a unique financial instrument that has both fixed income and growth characteristics. It is a bond that gives the investor the option to convert into common shares of the company.

A **bond** is a debt instrument issued by a company or a government. It pays interest, not dividends. The bond is an absolute obligation of the issuer. If a company cannot pay the interest on its bonds, the company will be declared bankrupt. Accordingly, bonds rank higher for safety than either preferred shares or common shares. Bonds pay a higher immediate return than common shares. In early 1995, corporate bonds yielded an average of 7% while stock dividends averaged around 2.5%. The difference is that corporations can deduct the bond interest expense from pre-tax income whereas stock dividend expense is deducted from after-tax income. There is a large bond market where securities are traded in the billions of dollars every day. The primary factors that affect bonds are the investment quality of the bonds, the interest rate they pay, the prime interest rate as set by the central bank, and general sentiment about future rates of inflation. Bonds are very vulnerable to changes in the prime interest rate. The reason is that the interest rate payable on the bond is fixed and will not change during the life of the bond. If the central bank raises interest rates, and banks follow suit, the market value of a bond will fall. If the central bank lowers interest rates and banks follow suit, the market value of a bond will rise. If I knew precisely what would happen to interest rates, I could make an uncountable fortune in the bond market.

■ Bond Yield

Bond yield is the rate of income return from the money invested taking into consideration the purchase price, the interest rate, and the duration of time until the bond matures. For example, at a price of 100, a 7% bond due in ten years will yield 7%. If the bond is purchased at 94, the yield to maturity would be 7.9%. This is calculated by combining two things: the amount invested is $940, so there will be a capital gain of $60 when the bonds matures at 100. To this is added $70 received annually as interest.

The greatest enemy of the bond is inflation. As inflation looms, interest rates rise. The value of a bond falls until its yield to maturity matches the current bank interest rate. For example, if a bond pays an interest rate of 8%, and banks are offering 12% on savings, then the bond is not sellable at the full value of 100. The bond must fall in price until it is also yielding 12%, which means it would have to drop to approximately 66 - (8/12) to be competitive with what the banks are offering. On the other hand, let's suppose during a period of deflation, bank interest rates fall. The bank is offering savers 3% on a savings account. The person holding a bond paying 8% is looking good. The price isn't 100 anymore, either. Why should the investor sell his bond for such a low price? The bond price will rise until it is currently yielding 3%, which is around 266 - (8/3). These figures are only ballpark numbers as other factors such as when the bond is callable are important, too. However, we see that despite its "fixed" nature, there is such a thing as a capital gain or capital loss in the bond market.

■ Convertible Bond Structure

A convertible bond is a popular means of financing for corporations that do not wish to issue straight bonds because they require a very high interest rate. The corporation may also decide, for various reasons, not to issue more common shares because this will dilute the stock. The convertible bond can be sold with a lower interest rate by adding a feature that will interest investors. The conversion privilege is a "kicker" that says the investor can collect interest while taking part in the overall success of the corporation and any price appreciation in the stock. A convertible bond is attractive to the investor because it:

• provides a higher yield than common stock;

• ranks ahead of common and preferred shares for payment;

• has a greater potential for capital gain if the common shares rise;

• has the yield support of a fixed interest investment.

In an independent study, it was found that between 1988-1994, the total return for convertible bonds outperformed the composite of the underlying stocks they represented for five of the six years. Accordingly, if Dynamic Corporation offers both common shares and convertible bonds, the investor would be better off to buy the convertible bonds.

The convertible bond is convertible into a pre-specified number of common shares of the issuing company over a period of years. Each bond has a face value of $1,000 but prices are quoted in $100 denominations. The redemption feature allows the issuing company to call the bond back before maturity. A typical convertible bond has a three year non-call period, followed by an early call period of three years. If the bond is called during this period, the bondholder is often paid a bonus for having the bond called back so early. After this is the "hard" period during which the bond can only be called if the common stock trades at 125% of its face value for 20 consecutive days. Let's put all this information together using an actual example:

Cascades Inc. 7.25% August 19, 2003

Conversion: Convertible at $6.50 per share until August 19, 1998 and at $7.25 per share thereafter to maturity.

Redemption: Redeemable from August 19, 1996 up to and including August 19, 2000 at par plus accrued and unpaid interest, provided that the weighted average of the trading price of the common shares during the 20 consecutive trading days ending five days prior to the date on which notice of redemption is given exceeds 125% of the applicable conversion price.

Retraction: Retractable at the option of the holder on 45 days' notice on August 20, 1998 at par plus accrued and unpaid interest. The company may elect to pay the principal amount of the debentures by payment of the number of common shares obtained by dividing $1,000 by 95% of the weighted average trading price for the 20 consecutive trading days ending five trading days before August 20, 1998.

Cascades is a company that manufactures boxboard, linerboard, fine paper, and tissue paper. It is listed on the Toronto Stock Exchange and its earnings have improved markedly in the past two years.

The term **redemption** means that the company may call in the bonds and pay the holders according to the stated terms. **Retraction** means the holder may cash in the bond according to the stated terms.

We have to perform an important calculation at this point. The bond is convertible into stock at the rate of $6.50 per share until August 19, 1998, thereafter at $7.25. This means each $1,000 bond may be exchanged for 153.84 shares of common stock ($1,000/$6.50). This exchange ratio is very important for our real purpose in buying this particular bond. We want a high exchange ratio. If, for example, another bond allows exchange at $50 per share, this means each $10,000 bond can be exchanged for 200 shares of stock. This is not sufficiently attractive for option trading. If we purchase $10,000 of Cascades convertible bonds, they can be converted into 1,538 shares of common stock.

■ Bond Ratings

All bonds are not created equal. The value of a bond is also measured by the financial strength of the company that issued it. If the company is heavily in debt and may not be able to pay the interest on the bond, it should be avoided. Bond rating services study the balance sheets of bond issuers and award quality ratings. The two major services in Canada, Dominion Bond Rating Service and Canadian Bond Rating Service, use the following codes:

	DBRS	*CBRS*
Highest Investment Quality	AAA	A++
Superior Quality	AA	A+
Upper Medium Grade	A	A
Medium Grade	BBB	B++
Lower Medium Grade	BB	B+
Highly Speculative	CCC	C
In Default	CC	D

The present bond rating for Cascades is B+ from Canadian Bond Rating Service. This is not the highest rating, but is quite satisfactory. In case of bankruptcy, the convertible bond holder ranks behind creditors with specific claims on the company assets, but ahead of preferred and common shareholders.

◼ A Claim Upon Common Shares

The convertible bond is a claim upon the common shares. At the time of my initial bond purchase, I bought $50,000 of bonds paying 122 for them ($61,000). The common stock was trading at $7.25. If I immediately converted my bonds into stock, I would receive 8,000 shares ($50,000/$6.25) of common stock. This would have a market value of $58,000 (8,000 x $7.25). I would lose money by immediate conversion.

However, I believe that within two years, the stock can reach $8.50 per share. My hypothetical value would then be $$68,000 (8,000 shares x $8.50). So, if the stock does move up in price, I am gaining right along with it because my bond is a claim upon the common shares. This is a very attractive feature, one that somewhat reduces the problem of higher interest rates pounding down the price of a bond. If the stock moves up, the convertible bond will move up no matter what interest rates are doing.

Even in the absence of any other features, it's a nice investment.

◼ The Convertible Bond As A Bond

If the common shares of the corporation perform badly and drop in price, the convertible bond will react in the same manner. If the price of the common stock fell to $5.50 per share, then my bond value is only $44,000 (8,000 x $5.50). However, my bond may not fall that low. The reason is that it is still a bond. Assuming the quality of the bond is still good, then the yield the bond pays will create a floor under the price. The Cascades bond pays 7.25%. If banks and other similar bonds are paying the same rate, then my bond will fall no lower. Let's assume similar bonds are being sold on the bond market for 110. My bond will drop from 122 to 110, but no further. The conversion value has little or no importance now. My investment is trading as a straight bond. However, I suffered a smaller drop than the person who owns common shares.

■ The Convertible Bond and Margin

The margin requirement on bonds is much lower than for stocks. Bonds are a more secure investment, so the broker will lend more against them. The current requirement of most investment houses is 10% of par value plus 30% of any amount over par value. It is a bit of a contradiction that the higher the price of the bond, the less the broker will lend. As the bond might be called at par value of 100, the further it goes over par the less money the broker will lend against it. As I paid 122 for the Cascades bonds, the margin would be 10% of 100 and 30% of 22. This works out to $10 for the 100 and $6.60 for the 22. For the purchase of $10,000 in bonds, the margin should be $1,660, for $50,000 in bonds it is $8,300. This is not high, just a bit under 17% compared to 33% for stocks. And, as you can guess, the word "leverage" creeps in again. The investor can buy more bonds with the same amount of money as common shares.

■ Convertible Bonds As Optionable Securities

None of what I have discussed so far is the real reason to buy a convertible bond. The reason lies in the simple fact that a holder of a convertible bond has a claim upon the common shares of the company. The holder may convert and thereby "deliver" the common shares upon demand. This means that the holder of a convertible bond is really a common stock holder for all intents and purposes. There is no reason why the holder should not be allowed to sell calls as a covered write against those claimable shares. Returning to my $50,000 of Cascades convertible bonds, I could sell 80 calls because my bonds represent 8,000 shares. The call I chose is the January 1996 $8.00 call. I received $0.65 for them or a

total of $5,200. Now, I can calculate my return. It is
necessary to convert all figures to annual figures in order to
have a consistent result.

Interest on the bonds

$50,000 x 7.25% = $3,625 per year

Premiums received for calls

$5,200 for 8 months, or $7,800 annualized

Annual Return

$3,625 + $7,800 = $11,425

Margin interest paid to broker

$52,700 x 10.5% = $5,533

Profit

$11,425 - $5,533 = $5,892

Profit as a percentage

$5,982/$8,300 = 71%

We can look at this another way. I was required by my
broker to put up $8,300 cash to buy the bonds. I
immediately received $5,200 in call premiums. In reality, I
only had to put up $3,100 of my own money. My profit was
still $5,787 on an investment of $3,100 which raised my
profit percentage to 186%. However, I don't use this last
calculation because it starts to appear a bit contrived, but it
is quite correct in accounting terms. My calculation does not
include any price appreciation in the stock. I have added
only the bond interest and the call premiums. Let's suppose
that the stock moves from $7.25 to $8.00. This adds
additional value of $0.75 per share and I hold a claim upon
8,000 shares. This additional gain would be $6,000 and my
profit would increase to 133%.

I did not include any commissions, so you can knock a
few percentage points off these calculations. Admittedly,
there is no guarantee the common shares will perform this

well, but my opinion is that the paper industry is doing very well and that the common stock is undervalued. The company may earn $1.60 per share in 1996, which means it would be trading at a P/E ratio of 4.5:1 which is very cheap. I think interest rates will soon trend downwards and that will cost me less margin interest. No matter how you look at it, it's a good investment and this is an excellent way to play it.

Let's work through another example. In May 1995, Air Canada floated an 8% convertible debenture as part of a unit package with 200 shares of Class A non-voting stock. The debentures were later sold separately at par. The Class A stock was then trading at $5.00 while the common stock was trading at $5.75. The bond is convertible into 125 shares of the Class A stock. I bought $100,000 of the bonds and put up $10,000. The $100,000 in bonds give me a call upon 12,500 shares of Class A stock. The broker margined $90,000, charging me interest at 10.5%. I then sold 125 January calls on the common stock, exerciseable at $6 and received $0.65 for them. Technically speaking this was a naked call because I sold calls on a different security than the one I actually owned. This fact is of little significance as the class A shares and the common shares move in tandem. However, I sold short an equal number of Class A shares and established a "hedge" and did not have to put up further margin. (I realize this is getting somewhat complicated so I won't expand upon it much further.) The result of the positions I took was very profitable, yielding over 90%. However, as I put up only a small fraction of the cost of the bonds, my return was more than 300%.

I did not allow for many positive things that might take place. If interest rates trend down, the market value of the bonds will rise and my broker will charge me less interest on the margin account. If the stock does reasonably well, and I think it could rise to $7.50 in two years, this will help pull the bond value up significantly. Is Air Canada a safe investment? The prospectus that came with the offer stated that the company can cover its interest payments from its cash flow by a ratio of 1.4 times. Very few companies default on their bonds and the defaulters have most often been real estate development companies that were leveraged to crazy ratios. It is a statistical fact that only 2% of corporate bonds issued in the past 30 years have gone into default, and this includes the high-risk junk bonds issued by Michael Milken when he ran the investment company of Drexel Burnham. And, of those that defaulted, investors recovered 80% of their investment. Coverage of 1.4 times is well within industry standards.

It's that easy, and it just doesn't get any better than this.

■ It Takes A Bit Of Searching

The basic problem an investor encounters is a shortage of really good quality, high-exchange rate convertible bonds. There are approximately 60 in Canada and 200 in the United States. Some have low quality ratings. Some are exchangeable into a very small number of shares and aren't suitable for that reason. For others, there are no options sold on the options market. Options are the key to the strategy, so make *certain* there are options before buying the convertible debentures. However, there are good investment choices from solid companies, including Rogers Communications, John Labatt Ltd., Ivaco, Abitibi-Price, Agnico-Eagle Mines, Inco, Domtar, and others. The primary points to keep in mind are a sound investment in an established company, optionable shares, a debenture price not too far above par, and a high conversion rate of shares per debenture so you may sell a large number of calls.

Chapter 10

Technical Analysis

"Stocks do not take random walks nor follow perfect patterns."

The notion that a graphic portrayal of past stock price movements would help to predict future movements did not begin with Charles Dow, but he somehow acquired credit for it. The "chartist" as he or she was formerly called, is a person who believes that stock and market prices give readable "signals" about their future price movements. The computer has added considerably to the number crunching and has also increased the number of "technical indicators" that can be studied to determine if a stock is over-priced or under-priced and which direction it will move. For a number of years, the best-known of the technical indicators was "The Elves" on the television program *Wall Street Week*. Analyst Robert Nurock applied ten tests or indicators to the market and gave buy or sell signals whenever six or more indicators were positive or negative. In the 1980s, this method began to fail with considerable frequency. Nurock concluded that the size and financial power of the options market and computer trading was making his method unreliable. The Elves were dropped from the program in favour of asking ten technical analysts whether they are neutral, bullish or bearish.

Many successful investors consider technical analysis to be of no value. They are not persuaded that the past is any help in predicting the future. There are also investors who are devotees of the "Random Walk Theory" which asserts that stock price movements and market movements are completely unpredictable and that throwing a dart at a list of stocks will have the same rate of success as careful stock selection. I have always believed that this theory is completely without merit.

Technical analysis has a value. However, I do not advocate trading solely on the basis of charts. The "pure chartist" doesn't know what a company does. He or she merely buys and sells based upon the charts. This simply makes no sense and incorporates an element of unwanted danger.

Technical analysis plays an important role in my investment method in three ways: (1) it provides a pictorial history of the stock price movement that is clearer than simply reading numbers; (2) it assists me in picking suitable price levels to buy shares or sell options; and (3) it assists me in deciding when to add to an existing position.

I don't recommend keeping your own stock charts, although that is not particularly difficult. Charts are available from companies that specialize in producing them, and from your broker. The explanation and discussion of chart analysis which follows is admittedly simplified and does not begin to cover the enormous range of other techniques of analysis that exist.

■ Chart Constructions

The primary method of recording stock price movements is the bar chart. Each day, a vertical line is entered on graph paper extending from the highest price of the day to the lowest price of the day. The last trade of the day is shown by a horizontal line:

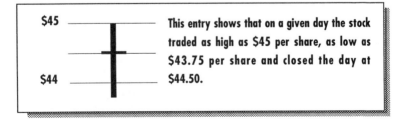

$45 ⎯⎯⎯⎯⎯ This entry shows that on a given day the stock traded as high as $45 per share, as low as $43.75 per share and closed the day at $44.50.

$44 ⎯⎯⎯⎯⎯

The lines on the graph paper are not evenly spaced. As the price rises, the lines are closer together because one of the purposes of the chart is to show percentage of change as well as dollar change. The space between $15 and $20 is greater than the space between $45 and $50 because a move from $15 to $20 would represent an increase of 33 percent, while a move from $45 to $50 would represent an increase of just 11 percent. For simplicity, I did not do this.

Most charts also show the number of shares traded each day (volume) as a vertical line at the bottom. Dow Theory holds that volume is an important indicator. If a stock rises on heavy volume (number of shares traded) this is regarded as more significant than if the stock rises on light volume. The increase in option trading has made this calculation less important and possibly misleading.

■ Channels

A chart may show that a stock has remained within a trading range for a lengthy period of time, but with a definite rising or falling trend. The trading range is called the stock's **channel** and indicates where buying tends to increase and where profit-taking has generally occurred. A channel patterns appears as follows:

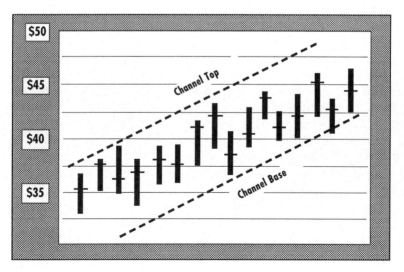

The standard belief is that the stock will remain in this channel until such time as it makes a definite, readable change of pattern, creating what is generally called a "breakout" on either the upside or the downside. The longer the stock remains in the channel, the longer it is likely to continue to do so.

A rising channel is a positive chart pattern. It shows that the stock is on a strong upward path with minor variations along the way. The technical analyst would predict that when the price reaches $46 or $47 per share, selling pressure will cause it to fall back to the base of the channel before buying resumes. Therefore, if the investor waits, he should be able to purchase shares around $42 or $43 per share which will be the new, rising base.

Turn the chart upside down and you will see a falling channel. This suggests that the stock is in a downward trend and that each bounce will be weaker than the previous one. This is a negative chart pattern and the stock should be avoided until such time as it changes course and clear leaves the channel.

■ Resistance and Support Lines

A chart can show in pictorial form price levels where substantial numbers of buyers either buy shares of a stock or sell them. This space is often referred to as the **trading range** of the stock. These lines are not forever, and the chartist looks for a change in the pattern. If the price of the stock goes higher than all previous attempts to penetrate the resistance line, this is called a **breakout**. If it falls lower than previous support levels, this is called a **breakdown**. Both signify that something major has changed regarding the sentiment of the stock. Some chartists do not regard a significant move out of the trading range as reliable unless it happens on heavy volume. If a stock stays within the upper and lower limits of the support lines for a long period of time, this is called a **long base**. The longer the base, the more significant it is when the price breaks out of the box.

These lines assist an investor in deciding where to place buy or sell orders. Such a chart would appear as follows:

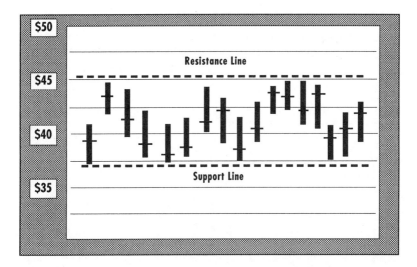

In this pattern, the stock price is caught in a trading range between $37.50 and $45.00. Whenever the price drops to the support line, buyers come into the market. However, when the price approaches $45, they sell. As long as this pattern persists, the investor should try to buy shares near the $37.50 mark. More importantly, the chart also suggests that calls sold exerciseable at $50 are very unlikely to be exercised.

■ Head And Shoulders

This pattern is regarded by many chartists as one of the most reliable predictors of future price movement. The pattern in the following chart suggests that the stock is unable to maintain its former upward momentum. The left shoulder shows the first time the stock ran into selling pressure. It then made a second effort (the head) and reached a new high, before falling back. On the third effort, the stock failed to reach or exceed the second effort. This forms the right shoulder. This is a very negative pattern, suggesting that the stock has run out of steam and that buyers are noticeably absent. If you draw a line along the bottom of the two shoulders, you create what is called "the neckline." If the stock falls below the neckline after completing the right shoulder, the chartist now anticipates a major decline in the price. Stock patterns sometimes set up a series of head and shoulder patterns, each formation lower than the preceding one. This will go on until the stock pattern changes. A head and shoulders looks like this:

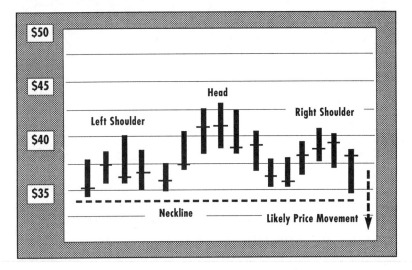

If we invert the chart, we produce a very positive pattern. The same factors are at work, but in reverse. The stock drops forming the left shoulder. It recovers somewhat, but drops again to an even lower level, forming the head. It recovers and declines once more, but not reaching the previous lows of the head. This suggests that the selling pressure is just about spent and that the stock will move higher, breaking the neckline on the upside. Some chartists advise that the investor should wait until the price movement has clearly broken the neckline, not merely anticipate that it will. However, this movement sometimes occurs very sharply and the stock price will jump out of the pattern.

The reverse head and shoulders sometimes is so smooth that it is not possible to really make out the three parts. Chartists call this a "saucer bottom" as it resembles the gradual curve of a saucer. A reverse head and shoulders pattern would appear as follows:

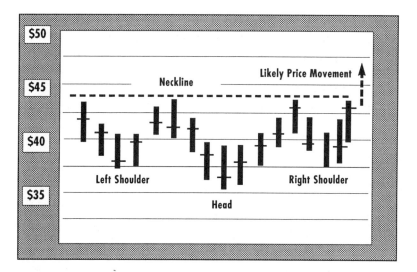

■ Pennants

One of the most reliable formations is called a **pennant**. A rising pennant suggests the stock price will soon move upwards. A declining pennant indicates a downward move. The pennant is formed by the trading range constantly getting narrower. In the bullish rising pennant shown below, the support line keeps rising, pushing against the resistance line which will eventually give way:

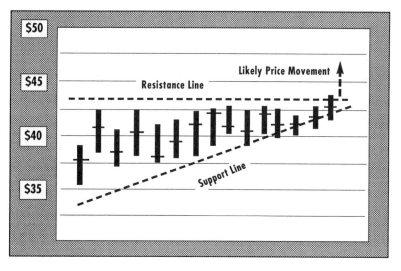

The rising pennant pattern is very positive and a breakout on the upside is the most likely direction.

If you turn the pennant chart upside down, you will see the exact opposite effect. The support line is the bottom line, and the resistance line keeps dropping lower and lower. This is "squeezing" the price action into a tighter and tighter corner of the triangle, but the momentum is clearly down. Eventually the stock will break down and fall below the resistance line.

■ Actual Chart Patterns

What I have discussed so far is theory. If it never actually occurs, then it is obviously of little use. Let's examine the charts of two stocks, General Electric and Wells Fargo. The scale has been reduced somewhat to get more information on the page. I have also deleted the closing cross bar so the vertical lines are easier to read. In the next chart for General Electric, how many patterns can you identify?

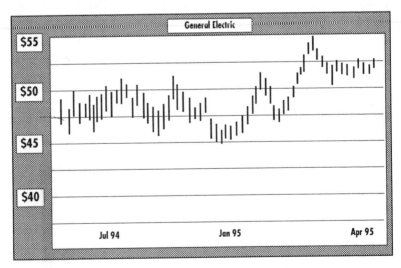

Let's look at the same chart again, with the various patterns marked upon it.

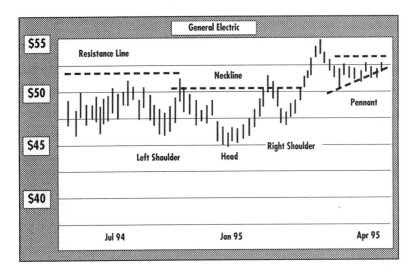

The stock shows three distinct patterns. It traded in a channel between $46 and $53. It then formed a reverse head and shoulders pattern, although not a particularly distinct one. It broke above the neckline in February 1995, indicating a sharp rise was likely. This ran out of steam rather quickly, however, around $55 a share in late February. It then settled down just below $50 and began trading in a narrow range, with an upward bias. This is the bullish pennant with the rising support line. In theory, the stock's next move would be upward again as it breaks out of the pennant. Did it? Yes. In May 1995, it moved to $58 per share before running into resistance again.

So, with this particular security, it did not give any false signals, which can happen.

If charts serve as a tool to predict price movements, what is the best use of that information? Charts help make three decisions: (1) buying shares; (2) selling calls; and (3) selling puts. When I saw the reverse head and shoulders pattern developing, it was a reasonable time to purchase shares at $48. It would be prudent to add more around $52 as the pennant was completing its formation. It was evident very early that the stock had great support around $45. Therefore, puts sold at this level were almost certain to be a good speculative bet. Even if the stock dropped below $45, and the puts were exercised, the worst thing that could happen is that I would be able to buy shares of GE with an average cost of just over $42. Considering the quality of the company that would be an excellent buy.

Having purchased shares at $48, I chose $55 as the point where I sold my covered calls. The stock doesn't make movements much greater than $7 at a time before selling comes in and it settles down in a narrow trading pattern for a while:

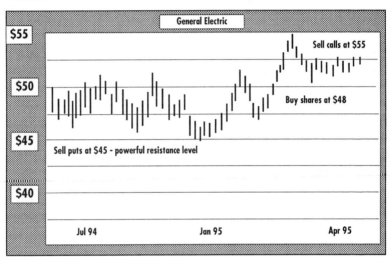

As a second example, study the following chart for Wells Fargo. This rather high-priced stock is one of the largest financial institutions in the western United States and has benefitted from a building resurgence after a series of natural disasters in California coupled with a recession. There are distinct patterns in this chart as well, but this time I will not provide them for you graphically. You should be able to see them. As you study the chart, first try to determine where you would sell a put. This would be a position where the likelihood of the stock dropping any lower is very limited. Next, assuming you purchased shares of the stock, where would you sell calls?

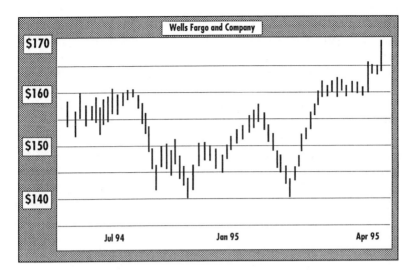

The most obvious point is that the stock has tremendous support at $140! It tested this level three times and each time new buying came in. That would be an excellent point to try to buy shares. Another strategy would be to sell puts at $135 and $140, which I did. I purchased shares at $143, sold calls at $150, but later had to buy the calls back and roll the position to $160. The stock went quickly above that level, making it necessary to roll my position again. (Something of a nuisance as I dislike having to roll my position too often.) However, I sold more puts at $150 which were very profitable.

■ Summing Up

Charts are not a substitute for fundamental research. I still want to know what the company's prospects and look for three good reasons why I should invest in that particular company. Having made the decision to invest in a company, the charts help me decide how and at what price level to enter the market. Once I determine a support level, I place puts at or below that level. I also know where I want to buy more shares. Resistance levels tell me where my covered call positions should be placed. It doesn't work every time, and I have to be prepared to alter course if the chart patterns prove to be wrong. However, they are more often right than wrong.

It is also important to keep in mind how many investors are chartists. A chart movement can become a self-fulfilled prophecy. A stock may go up, not because there is a fundamental reason that it should, but because so many chartists believe it will and immediately buy it. The cry of "Breakout! Breakout!" is a most pleasant sound to the investor who owns a particular stock that technicians have suddenly identified as a winner.

Chapter 11

Record Keeping

"A tax delayed is a tax saved."

The income tax laws of Canada and the United States have become so complex, they are a disgrace. It is embarrassing that the citizenry tolerates this extraordinary form of abuse. I filed my first tax return in the United States in 1958. It was a small card. On one side was space for my personal information, statement of income and names of any dependents. On the reverse side was a simple tax chart from which I calculated what I owed after deductions. The completion process took five minutes. I kept this simple tax return as a souvenir of a saner time.

What has happened? There are three factors that have made taxes unfair and unintelligible. The first is the mistaken belief that the economy of a nation can be improved by tinkering with the tax system. The second is the fascination of politicians with bestowing goodies upon select groups by altering tax rules. The third is the errant determination that taxes must be progressive.

The gifted hands of politicians have created a hopeless quagmire of tax laws and regulations that are incomprehensible to everyone. This has also given rise to an army of accountants, tax processors and collectors. The tax system changes so often that it is impossible for anyone to write a "current" tax book. It is out of date before the ink dries.

Therefore, I cannot spell out just how your option trading will be taxed. Canada has eliminated its capital gains exemption and the United States treats long-term gains and short-term gains differently. You must employ the services of a competent tax accountant or lawyer. My discussion will centre around the records you should keep for your own interest and for tax preparation.

I strongly advise against investing in anything because it comes with some sort of tax writeoff or benefit. That is not a valid reasons to enter into any investment. At one time, there were some very solid investments available with equally good tax avoidance features. However, governments have closed down most of these investments and what remains is seldom worthy.

■ Capital Gains Or Income

The majority of investors will have their option transactions treated as capital gains or losses. The taxable portion depends upon the tax laws in effect at the time. Capital losses can usually be used to offset capital gains in the same transaction year, or in some situations the preceding year or any subsequent taxation year.

Some investors will have all their transactions in options treated as income, not capital gains. Investors who fall into this category are:

- Any taxpayer who holds himself out to the public as a trader or dealer in securities.

- Any taxpayer whose course of conduct indicates the carrying on of a securities business, by virtue of the fact that he is buying and selling securities extensively for short periods of ownership and where the transactions form a major part of the taxpayer's business.

■ Taxation Of Covered Call Options

The taxation of a covered call option depends upon what happens at the expiration date. Keep separate records for stocks and options even though they might eventually become joined. The following is a general outline of how the government treats covered option writing:

• When the call option is written, it is treated as a capital gain in the taxation year in which it is written.

• If the call option is exercised in a subsequent year, the writer must file an amended tax return for the taxation year in which the option was written excluding the capital gain from income. Then, the premium is added to the sale proceeds in the subsequent taxation year when computing the capital gain or loss on the disposition of the underlying stock.

• If the call option is closed out by the purchase of an offsetting position (rolling the option) the cost of acquiring the offsetting option is treated as a capital loss in the taxation year in which the option is closed out.

• If the call option expires, it is treated as a capital gain with a cost of zero.

■ Taxation Of Put Options

Puts are taxed in a similar manner. Generally, when the put option is sold, it is treated as a capital gain in the taxation year in which the put option is written. Other rules include the following:

• If the put option is exercised in a subsequent year, the seller must file an amended return for the taxation year in which the put option was written excluding the capital gain from income. Then, the price of buying the shares is reduced by the put premium to obtain the adjusted cost price.

• If the put option expires worthless, treat it as a capital gain with a cost of zero.

■ Individual Stock Records

Record keeping is time consuming and takes away from time better spent analyzing stock opportunities. However, some record keeping is important to have an accurate position on how an investment is performing. The use of a computer spreadsheet program makes the process quick once the sheet is set up. If you don't have a computer, columnar accounting forms will serve the purpose.

A single page or file can reveal at a glance the present state of an investment along with its historic record. If you trade in markets in more than one country, you must decide how you are going to convert currencies. The tax department will accept one of two methods: (1) convert every transaction when it occurs; or (2) use an average conversion rate for the year. My most common conversion is between the Canadian dollar and the U.S. dollar. It is simple to put a currency conversion "cell" on the spreadsheet.

You should also keep accurate records of interest paid on your margin account and on tax-deductible bank loans. A file for a single stock could be set up as follows:

Giant Corporation

Date	Transaction	Share Purchase	Share Sale	Option Purchase	Option Sale	Dividend
Apr 19	Bot 500 shares	$27,678				
Apr 19	Sold 5 calls Sept 55				$1,897	
May 11	Bot 500 shares	$27,363				
May 11	Sold 5 calls Sep 55				$1,651	
Jun 10	Dividend					$200
Totals		$55,041			$3,548	$200

The individual record for a security provides at a glance the complete history of transactions and permits evaluation as to whether the security is performing well.

■ Summary Of Stock Trading

Records of stock transactions for tax purposes must show cost, sale and commissions paid. The required information is as follows:

| Stock Trading Summary 19-- | | | | | |

PURCHASES

Date Purchased	Security	No. Shares	Cost	Commission	Total Cost
May 9	Giant Corp	500	$25,500	$403	$25,903
Jun 15	Mythical Corp	500	$16,550	$293	$16,843
Totals			$42,050	$696	$42,746

SALES

Date Sold	Security	No. Shares	Proceeds	Commission	Total Gain or Loss
Sep 11	Giant Corp	500	$30,500	$420	$4,177
Totals			$30,500	$420	$4,177

The gain on the sale of 500 shares of Giant Corporation was calculated by the following formula: Total Cost – Proceeds – Commission (on sale) = Gain. Using dollar figures, the calculation is $30,500 – $420 – $25,903 = $4,177.

If additional shares of the same security are purchased over a period of time, it is necessary to constantly change the total cost to reflect the adjusted average cost. For example, if Investor K purchased 500 shares of Giant Corporation at $50 per share plus commission (total $25,500) then purchased another 500 shares at $56 per share plus commission (total $28,600) the total adjusted cost is $54,100 for 1,000 shares. His average cost per share is $54.10. If Investor K then sold 500 shares, he must use an adjusted cost for the 500 shares of $54.10 x 500 = $27,050. The point to be emphasized is that the calculation is not similar to the accounting term of "first in - first out." Investor K did not sell the first 500 shares he bought. He sold 500 shares from his total pool of 1,000. If Investor K later purchases another 500 shares at $45 per share, he must average this new pool with his existing pool which has an adjusted cost of $54.10. The new adjusted cost would be $49.55 ($45.00 + $54.10)/2.

The use of a computer spreadsheet allows the investor to write a simple program that performs the adjusted cost calculation automatically. If the investor trades in U.S. or other foreign stocks, an exchange value for the Canadian dollar vs. the U.S. dollar can be entered as a constant. Eventually, all figures must be in Canadian dollars for tax purposes.

■ Summary Of Option Trading

I prefer to show sales of options first, because I always sell puts and calls. I may or may not purchase them back at a later date:

Option Trading Summary 19--					
SALES					
Date Sold	Security	Options	Proceeds	Commission	Total Proceeds
Sep 9	Giant Corp	5 calls Mar 35	$2,250	$ 90	$2,160
Sep 11	Mythical Corp	5 calls Mar 25	$1,500	$ 80	$1,420
Mar 17	Giant corp	5 calls Sep 40	$2,500	$100	$2,400
Mar 19	Mythical Corp	5 calls Sep 30	$2,000	$ 85	$1,915
Totals			$8,250	$355	$7,895
PURCHASES					
Date Bought	Security	Options	Cost	Commission	Total Gain or Loss
Mar 21	Giant Corp	5 calls Mar 35	0	Expired	$2,160
Feb 20	Mythical Corp	5 calls Mar 25	$1,100	$ 80	$ 240
Totals			$1,100	$ 80	$2,400

The Mar 35 calls for Giant Corporation expired worthless, so the investor sold 5 calls Sep 40. In February, the investor noted that the calls for Dynamic were now in the money and that if he took no action he would be called. He decided to buy back the Mar 25 calls for Dynamic Corporation and then sold 5 Sep 30 calls. For tax purposes for the year, the investor must report $2,400 as a capital gain. The other contracts are still open and the gain cannot be calculated until they are closed.

—————— **Chapter 12**

Investment Management

"The person who grabs the newspaper each day to check the price of his favourite stock as instant confirmation of his sound judgment is not well-suited for investing."

Many otherwise capable investors and money managers fall down when it comes to the all-important task of managing a portfolio, no matter how big or small. These individuals have a keen eye for bargains and seem to make sound purchases, but lack the constancy needed to keep the ship on course. Investments will not look after themselves. They need supervision and a constant flow of information.

It is not necessary to become a slave to the process. I would suggest that the minimum time commitment is two hours a week. There are some special periods when more time is required. Income tax preparation is such an instance.

At the same time, it is important to add to your knowledge. There are numerous sources of information. Much information is of little or no value and some is suspect. There is a danger in information-overload. In the United States, it is possible to watch financial news on television 24 hours a day. This is neither necessary nor healthy. However, when a stock rises or falls sharply, it is important to know why. When news commentators refer to an upcoming Consumer Confidence Report, it is somewhat reassuring to know what that means. If your investment management is taking too much time, you are doing something wrong. You may have purchased too many different securities or are trading too much. It is important to feel in control and aware of what you hold at all times. This is true whether it is a portfolio worth $10,000 or $10 million.

■ Sources Of Information

Information comes in infinite forms. I generally divide investment information into two groups: general sources and current sources. Current sources refers to price movements and news items that might affect my securities. General sources includes books and articles that discuss investment concepts, trends and attitudes. Devote some time to both. I will begin by discussing the second category, as it is the smaller one.

General Sources

It is helpful to read some of the classics of investing written by individuals who acquired great financial success and also avoided colossal ruin. Some of these works are not recent, but most libraries still have them. I highly recommend as general works, *The Battle for Investment Survival*, by Gerald Loeb and *The Intelligent Investor*, by Benjamin Graham. Loeb was known as the Dean of Wall Street for many years, and Graham was the guru of value investing. Graham stressed that investors should forget the hype and look at the balance sheet. He once said, "Even the liabilities should be solid!"

If you are very enthusiastic about increasing your knowledge, and your wealth, then I recommend you enroll in an investment course. The best one is demanding and time-consuming, but it has no equal. The course is called the Canadian Securities Course. It is the course any person who wishes to be licensed as a financial adviser or broker must complete in order to apply for a licence. The cost is around $400. There is a long course and a short course. Information is available from the Canadian Securities Institute, 121 King Street W., Suite 1550, Toronto, Ontario, M5H 3T9. When you complete this course, you will be soundly versed in every aspect of investing. There is an examination, but you don't have to write it unless you intend to apply for a licence.

I recommend two books about the sages of the twentieth century. Peter Lynch's *Beating The Street* is very informative as is *The Warren Buffet Way* by Robert Hagstrom.

Current Sources

Let's begin with newspapers. Daily newspapers have a business section that contains prices and articles. However, the news section relates to your investments, too. If you own shares of Philip Morris, and the U.S. Congress passes a bill limiting liability suits in the United States, then it will not surprise you to see the shares of Philip Morris rise.

The *Financial Post* is dedicated to investment news, but it also contains broader articles with a bigger horizon than just day-to-day events. It is good to think about what will happen five years from now as well as what will happen tomorrow. The trend-setting *Wall Street Journal* is available in Canada, but tends to arrive somewhat late. Our postal system doesn't seem to move financial news with the same speed as junk mail.

Financial magazines are very numerous and each has its own loyal following. *Forbes, Fortune, Financial World*, and *Business Week* are the best known, but there are good smaller publications such as *Money. Canadian Business* is more relevant to people whose investments are mainly in Canada, but I have personally not found the magazine to be particularly useful in making specific investment decisions.

Your best source of specific investment advice is your stock broker. His or her firm will either produce its own research reports or purchase them from an independent publisher. My broker's firm publishes Canadian research, and also has full access to a large New York firm's publications. These reports are either industry-based or company-based. They are prepared by analysts who specialize in particular fields and who recommend investors buy, hold, or sell certain securities. Don't accept these recommendations blindly. They are only opinions, and there are disclaimers printed on them reminding the investor of that status. Let your broker know the types of investments and companies that interest you. Don't waste their money and your time requesting a copy of everything.

There are specialized, independent subscription services that prepare detailed reports. The best known, and a company with a good reputation is Value Line, Inc., 220 E. 42nd Street, New York, NY 10017-5891. This company publishes reports on more than 1700 companies, most in the United States and Canada. Each page is crammed with data and commentary. There are also industry reports and special features. For example, when I read in *Value Line* in 1989 that Coca Cola was expanding the number of vending machines in Europe, I was puzzled as to why this was significant. *Value Line* explained that in the United States there is a Coca Cola vending machine for every 120 people, but in Europe, there is a machine for every 2,000 people. The potential sales increase in Europe was terrific. I also read that Warren Buffet was accumulating a huge block of Coca Cola stock. (His company presently owns 93 million shares!) There is another unique feature of *Value Line* that I admire. For whatever reasons, the company has an uncanny ability to predict future corporate earnings. Independent studies have confirmed that they are very accurate in these predictions. *Value Line* then uses the traditional Price/Earnings ratio and other factors to forecast a future price for the company. For example, General Electric has an average annual P/E ratio of 13:1. In the period 1997-1999, *Value Line* predicts the company will earn $5.50 per share. Therefore, the stock should be trading around $71.50 per share. It is presently at $56 per share. Lastly, *Value Line* assigns two numerical ratings to companies. There is a number for Timeliness and a number for Safety. The highest rating is a "1" and the lowest is a "5." A stock rated 1/1 is the highest rating available. A 5/5 should be avoided like the plague. Unfortunately, I have never found this rating system very good. My experience is that *Value Line* is too slow to change its ratings. It keeps a company at a high rating long after its fortunes have declined, and won't upgrade a company until all the real price gains have been made. When gold peaked at $800 in the 1980s, then began falling like an meteor, *Value Line* kept rating gold mining companies as 1/1 for months until investors had suffered a blood bath. The rating system is interesting, but don't rely very much upon it. As a caveat, *Value Line* is rather expensive. However, it is fairly said that if you get one good investment idea a year from their material, it was well worth the cost.

As you will be trading options, I would also recommend a report service called *Option Guide*, published by Daily Graphics, Inc., Box 66919, Los Angeles, California. This weekly service contains graphs and data about earnings and options prices. The company uses a computer to spot unusually high premiums on puts and calls and prints these as a separate list.

You have probably received in the mail or from someone else, an investment newsletter. There are thousands of them. There is even a newsletter that evaluates the newsletters. Typically, the writers of the newsletters use a series of technical indicators to advise subscribers what to buy and sell and when. The publishers tend to make exaggerated claims as to their success. I have never found them useful or profitable. I have always felt that if anyone was so infallible in the world of investing, that person would have so much money that there would be no reason whatsoever to publish a newsletter. My advice is to ignore them.

A recent comer to the world of information is television. *Wall Street Week* has a large following and is one of PBS's most popular programs. PBS scored a second coup by sponsoring *The Nightly Business Report* which provides information five nights a week. These programs are both interesting and instructive and are a better use of your time than watching tired sitcoms or another police show. In the United States, there are TV channels such as CNBC that broadcast financial news 18 hours per day. Some viewers are totally addicted to this channel. My view is that this is overkill and won't add to your success.

I want to add one more source. It is helpful to listen to people, particularly seniors. During my failed tour as a broker, I gleaned a unique bit of wisdom from a client of mine that he called "Noggin." Cardy, then in his eighties, had seen it all. He was particularly articulate in talking about the Great Depression. As a paint salesman, he wasn't making much money during the 1930s. In fact, he owed his company money because they paid him advances on his sales commissions and he wasn't selling any paint. His wife once asked if he thought his company would fire him, and he replied, "Not now. I owe them too much money." When World War II broke out, he was too old to enlist, but he thought about what the war would mean to the Canadian economy. Some investors quickly bought shares of steel companies, because a war requires steel. But Cardy knew more about war than most people. He bought for a few pennies a share the depressed stock of a then-closed paper mill in Quebec. He also bought shares of his own paint company. He told me that his "Noggin" said you can't fight a war without paper or paint. He was so very correct and reaped enormous profits. Coincidentally, he received the first big order for paint from the Canadian government.

Another interesting client was Charlie, a retired house painter. He had little formal education but a feel for the world. He was also an astute investor. When British Prime Minister Ted Heath got into a brawl in 1974 with striking coal miners, and called a needless election, all the polls showed that Heath would win. This gave investors reassurance because they saw the Labour Party as radical and dangerous, particularly towards the North Sea oil development. My clients and I had very substantial investments in the oil companies exploring the North Sea and very much feared a Labour Party victory. Heath campaigned vigorously by sailing on his yacht every day. This was a wonderful image — the millionaire playboy on his yacht while coal miners went hungry and people were cold. The polls said Heath was a sure thing, but Charlie insisted he would lose. He railed that Heath was a man who didn't care about nor understand ordinary people and he was flaunting that fact. He startled me by saying that even if people agreed with Heath, they would back the miners. I found that forecast hard to believe and clung confidently to my holdings. I should have listened to Charlie and sold my North Sea oil stocks. Heath lost mightily and my investment was duly pummeled.

■ You And Your Broker

The relationship between the investor and his or her broker is one that must be constantly reinforced and evaluated. I am fortunate that I first met my broker when I joined the same firm more than 25 years ago. He was from the "old school" and had begun as a chalk boy who marked the prices on the boards before the advent of electronics. He worked "in the cage" where stock and bond certificates are transferred and has a good "feel for the tape" meaning he senses how the market is behaving just from the action. More importantly, he's totally honest and provides me with the service I want.

As both a client and a former broker, I have a grasp of what makes a good working relationship.

It is essential that both investor and broker know what the investor is trying to do. The "Know your client rule" should be expanded to include "Client, know thyself." The investor's objectives, preferences, and goals should be clearly understood. For example, if the client is retired and needs income, then the broker should not suggest buying shares of a growth company that pays no dividends. At the same time, the client should not call up the broker and ask for an opinion on such a company because his cousin Larry says it's a hot issue.

Call your broker no more than once a day, and preferably around the same time. He or she will learn to expect your call and have current information available just for your portfolio. Don't call every ten minutes to ask for prices. They don't change that much. Avoid calling just as the market opens or just before it closes. Those times can be a bit hectic. If you are undergoing a major portfolio revision, you may have to make more calls than one, but that should not become habit. Some people want to call their broker just to chat. It's fine to put a few social comments into the conversation, but it's a business line, not a personal line. My broker can bring me up to date on what important news is on the wire service in less than two minutes. He seldom calls me, because my manner of investing doesn't involve snap decisions or panic selling. Don't be a "nuisance account," a term that refers to an investor who asks for tons of information but never buys or sells anything. The bottom line is that the broker lives on commissions. The client who talks and talks, wants every research report available, and does nothing is a nuisance.

I want to take to task writers who make disparaging remarks about brokers. Just as the legal profession wonders why lawyers are so abused verbally and in print, brokers are not pleased by crude and unwarranted insults. Like any profession, some are incompetent and a few are dishonest. That can never be eliminated, but that does not excuse statements which I have recently read in books and articles, such as, "A broker is someone who invests your money until it's his" and "Ten things your broker doesn't want you to know." These writers are predictably extolling the wonders of mutual funds and their own newsletters. It is not necessary to take cheap shots at very professional people to do so. When I was a broker, I never abused the trust of a client. Sometimes my clients made profits, sometimes not. But, to imply that I was bilking them for my own benefit is completely false, and I never knew any other broker to do so. A recent book on mutual funds (one of the worst bits of drivel I've ever read) attacked brokers as incompetent charlatans and added this challenge: "Did you ever meet a person who made any money in the stock market?" My answer, if I bothered to respond, would be, "Yes, Cardy, Charlie, and me."

■ Reviewing Your Portfolio

I completely upgrade all the information in my portfolio once a month. The computer spreadsheet is a great help. I evaluate each security's performance and check off those that are doing exactly what I want. I print out the list of options sorted by expiry month. I don't want to overlook a call that is in-the-money and have the stock called away. I prepare a list of possible changes I might make and look at my cash position carefully.

Once a year, this process undergoes a more extensive review. I do this in early December because if I am going to sell a loser, this must be done in time to claim a capital loss for the year. The sale must be done at least five trading days before the end of the month or the actual transaction date will be in January. This annual ritual is affectionately called **Tax loss selling**.

I file brokerage reports, *Value Line* reports, and articles in separate folders for each security. I review them frequently and go through the "three good reasons" exercise. Those that fail are weeded out. A stock may be sold not because it has done badly, but because it has done too well. It may have risen to such a high price that it is now over-priced and doesn't justify the high P/E ratio. I spend no more than three hours a week actually reading research material and reviewing my holdings. There is no need to do more because you are not learning anything new.

■ Playing A Winning Hand

Several years ago, someone asked me what was the most important part of my investment strategy. I replied, "I absolutely refuse to lose money." I did not intend the answer to sound flippant, but merely implied that a dogged determination to develop a winning plan and stick to it was the most important decision I made.

I have probably made, or seen, every portfolio management mistake known. I have tried to eliminate them over the years, but eternal vigilance is needed. Although it is prudent to diversify and not put all your money into one security, most people have too many stocks. An individual can properly keep track of no more than eight or ten securities. Yet, I have met people holding thirty or more. What usually happens is ten go up, ten go down, ten go sideways. The end result is zero. You cannot do a thorough job of managing so many holdings. I recently read the annual report of a small mutual fund, with a total value of $20 million. The fund had invested in more than 800 stocks! The manager could not possibly know anything about so many companies. I also noted that he had purchased as few as 65 shares of one company. For what possible purpose? Don't duplicate investments. Don't buy Coca Cola *and* Pepsi Cola. You need not own shares of Ford *and* General Motors.

It is important to discount the argument that you can't do it yourself, that professionals dominate the markets, and small investors will be eaten up. Nothing could be more wrong. The most common form of professional investing is the open-end mutual fund. It offers professional management to the small investor, and should deliver upon that promise. Yet, a surprising number of funds fail to equal the market averages. There is an explanation for that problem and it underlies the basic weakness of investment funds. Professional investors and fund managers are required to report to their clients or shareholders quarterly. Clients expect good results every quarter and quickly abandon ship at the first hint of trouble. This forces professional managers to become stock chasers. They go through a quarterly ritual known as **portfolio window dressing** which means selling those investments that are below their purchase prices, regardless of quality and potential. The fund manager wants to appear infallible and sells good securities even though he or she believes that the market prices are only temporarily depressed. To do otherwise is to encourage "financial desertion" by shareholders. This leads to the second problem fund managers must face — the dreaded redemptions. In theory, when a fund shareholder invests his or her money, the shareholder wants the fund manager to do the thinking. If market conditions look bearish, the manager might decide to sell some securities, raise some cash, or perhaps move into T-bills. The shareholder need not worry or sell shares because the manager is taking care of business. So much for the theory. In actual practice, the plan does not work. Shareholders read the financial papers and watch the news. When the reports turn bearish, the shareholders stampede and begin bailing out of the funds. This redemption flood is much like a run on a bank and forces fund managers to sell securities in order to pay off the shareholders. In severe bear markets, mutual funds have been forced to sell just about everything — the good, the bad, and the ugly — at the very moment when they would prefer to be buying. The basic, underlying weakness of the open-end mutual fund is that it is never its own boss. It is always held hostage to the moods and whims of the shareholders who can suddenly take their money off the table and play havoc with the manager's strategy. This does not happen to the individual investor who does not have to report to anyone and who has full control over whether he or she will buy, sell, or hold. There is no better argument in favour of managing your own investment portfolio than the simple fact that you don't have to impress anyone. As a reminder of this industry's problems, in the first six months of 1995 only 12% of the stock mutual funds beat the S&P, with the average rund achieving a total return on just 16%. And, this lipid performance occurred during a period when the overall stock market recorded extraordinary growth with the S&P rising 20%. Consider also that the funds that had the best performance were dominant in just one sector of the market — the high tech stocks. This is not a performance likely to be repeated.

If you have built up a surplus of cash, and cannot find any new investment ideas, the obvious place to look is your present portfolio. Add more shares of your winning ideas. Don't be put off by the fact that you bought your present shares at a lower price. Everything is relative. I bought shares of General Electric when it earned $2 per share. I bought more, at a higher price, when it earned $4 per share. This is not important. What is important is that when I bought the shares at the higher price, the P/E ratio was actually lower and the dividend yield higher. That is, in terms of relative value, I got a better bargain at the higher price. A person could argue that if he bought shares of General Electric thirty years ago, he got a better price than I did. That doesn't mean a thing. You're buying for the future, not the past. I might buy more shares of GE ten years from now at triple the price it is today. That will be a mistake only if the earnings are not keeping pace and the P/E is too high. Price your purchases rather than time them. If an investment looks inexpensive and the rewards promising, the right time to buy is now. In the short term the stock may dip a bit, but if you chose real value, it won't drop by much. Trying to get the absolute lowest price on a stock never works. I want to stress the value point vigorously. Some stocks trade at prices which make no sense. Boston Chicken is a good company, but when it went public on the first day it was bid up to 150 times earnings. A major investment house recently urged investors to buy shares of PetSmart with a P/E of 100:1. This makes no sense today, tomorrow, or anytime.

Stay fully invested 100% of the time. You can't time the market and you can't predict events. There is no reason to "raise cash" and "wait for the next correction" because no one knows if or when that will be. Don't let world events keep you out of the market. It is said that markets climb a "wall of worry." In the past 25 years, we saw an oil embargo, the S & L debacle, interest rates over 20 percent, the collapse of the Soviet Union, a war in Vietnam, the resignation of an American president, and gold at $800 an ounce. But, the Dow Jones Industrial Average quietly moved from 500 to 4800. Yet, on any given day, a bearish hand-wringer would have whined that the sky was falling and warned you not to invest. My favourite is a panelist on *Wall Street Week* who looks like a puppy that wet the carpet and grimaces when he says, "My indicators look r-e-a-l-l-y bad right now (Groan). The market looks r-e-a-l-l-y weak right here. (Whimper). I'm r-e-a-l-l-y worried." If that guy ever says things are looking bright, then I'll start to worry!

I keep a stock for an average of four years, but have held some for eight years. It is a mistake to sell a stock just because you are tired of it. It's not like changing your wardrobe or hair style. There is nothing wrong with the possibility that you might hold a high-quality security for the rest of your life.

Pay no attention to fraudulent theories such as the Random Walk Theory or the Efficient Market Theory which hold that at any given time stock prices are where they should be because the market has so many participants that it is 100% efficient. According to this theory, you can never do better than the crowd, so why try? The Nay-sayers argue that stocks don't have memories and therefore don't know their resistance lines or support lines. Maybe not, but smart investors know! Ignore those who tell you that you must buy mutual funds and that you cannot invest money yourself because you are competing against the pro's and the big guys

and can't get a fair deal. This is errant nonsense. There is
nothing a fund manager does that you cannot do. There are
ample studies that show that diligent attention paid to the
market, careful selection, and emphasis upon quality will
outperform the averages year after year. Warren Buffet told
his shareholders, "It is not necessary to do extraordinary
things to get extraordinary results." *Fortune* magazine
studied just four investment managers—Warren Buffet,
Charles Munger, Bill Ruane, and Walter Schloss. These men
have outperformed the market averages every year for more
than 30 years. The investment firm of Tweedy Brown has a
similar record of success back to 1959. Fortune concluded
that successful investors believe current prices are wrong.
They believe that the market is constantly overlooking great
value. They are not concerned with the present price, but
with the future price.

Perhaps a sports illustration will help. Roberto Clemente,
the great outfielder for the Pittsburgh Pirates, had the
game's best skill at playing a long ball off the wall. Hitters
who assumed they had an easy double were dismayed to be
thrown out at second by one of Clemente's rifle shots from
right field. Runners who were on second base and who loafed
around third base thinking they would score easily were
stunned to be thrown out at home plate by that same
incredible arm. Clemente's secret was that he never ran after
the ball. He figured out from the arch of the ball how it
would hit and bounce. He ran to where the ball would be and
waited for it. Successful investors do the same thing. They
figure out where the stock is going, get there early, and wait
for it.

I bought shares of Caterpillar when the company's
bottom line looked anemic. The management had finally
conceded that its main production line was ass-backwards,
inefficient, and hopeless. A part was made in Shed 1, taken
to Shed 2 where holes were drilled in it. It came back to Shed
1 for a primer coat. It went to Shed 3 for finishing paint. It
went back to Shed 1 for further assembly. Caterpillar
decided to spend nearly $1 billion and bulldoze the whole
stupid mess. The cost hit the profit and loss statement hard
and the union was most unhappy (and still is). But, the new

system cut costs by 40 percent and profits soared two years later, trouncing Cat's biggest rival, Japan's Komatsu, all over the world. Regrettably, serious labour problems at Caterpillar continue and they are holding the stock price down somewhat, but the company seems to be keeping its inventory up on schedule. There is an old adage, "Buy 'em when no one loves 'em." This is very wise advice indeed, IF you are confident some day they will love 'em.

Lastly, keep your eyes, ears, and nose open for ideas. Several years ago, my wife and I were in Ottawa and looking for a restaurant. We passed one that had a line of patrons outside and down the street. My first instinct was, "Don't go there. It's crowded. Look at the line!" Then my "Noggin" started buzzing and that's exactly where we went — to find out why all those people were standing in line. The establishment was one of the first Swiss Chalet restaurants. I learned that the chain is owned by Cara Foods, a company that also has the exclusive rights to prepare frozen meals for airplanes in Toronto and other cities. If people are willing to stand in line to get food while other restaurants are nearly empty, it's got to be a good investment. I bought shares of Cara Foods and made an excellent profit.

The Canadian company that acquired the exclusive rights to market Sony products in Canada got the contract by accident. The president was on an airplane and began talking to a somewhat dejected Japanese salesman who said he had been talking to Canadian companies about his company's product line, without success. The Canadian asked, "What do you make?" and the Japanese man showed him some of Sony's new products, including a prototype for the Walkman. The Canadian had the good presence of mind to recognize a jewel when he saw it. He said, "I'll sell your products," and signed the contract right there on the plane.

Sometimes money is talking straight at you so you keep your antennae up and use your "Noggin'."

It's that easy.

Stewart's 20 Investment Rules

1. Never buy or sell by formulas, percentages, or pre-determined price targets.

2. Investing begins with cost-cutting. Your standard of living must be reduced to provide a surplus of funds to invest.

3. The four pillars of investment are pension and retirement funds, insurance, cash, and growth. Don't sacrifice one for another.

4. Couples must work together and be mutually supportive of financial goals. A house divided will never prosper.

5. Develop a financial plan and stick to it. Change the plan only if conditions change. Don't change your portfolio just because you want a "new look."

6. Don't buy or hold any investment unless you can quickly cite three good reasons for doing so.

7. Don't invest in anything that causes you worry. Investing should be a positive part of your life, not one that produces stress.

8. Buy quality. Leave speculation to the other person.

9. Never borrow to purchase personal items. Borrow for investment purposes, because the interest is tax-deductible and you cannot earn enough money or live

long enough for compounding to work. Your mortgage can be tax deductible.

10. Sell covered options (calls) to increase your return on investment and reduce risk. Don't buy puts or calls or otherwise speculate in the options market.

11. Sell an underlying security (stock) only when something has fundamentally changed.

12. Average up, not down. Forget dollar cost averaging — it's a gimmick.

13. Don't try to time the market, you can't. Buy for price.

14. Don't try to predict interest rate movements. You can't.

15. Convertible bonds, combined with covered options, offer a high rate of return with less risk than stocks.

16. Keep accurate records for tax purposes and for you own analysis, but don't waste time constantly counting your profits.

17. Be patient. Few good investments produce immediate returns. Ignore short-term market fluctuations.

18. Find a good stock broker and a good tax accountant. If you don't have great confidence in them, look elsewhere.

19. Mutual funds are suitable for RRSP investment and for investors who don't want the responsibility of decision making. Mutual funds, however, are not superior to your own personal investing.

20. Don't invest in anything you don't understand.

Appendix 2

Glossary Of Investment Terms

ACCRUED INTEREST   Interest accumulated on a bond since the last interest payment date.

ASSETS   Everything a corporation or a person owns or is owed.

AVERAGING DOWN   Buying more of a security at a lower price than the original investment to reduce the average cost per unit.

AVERAGING UP   Buying more of a security at a higher price than the original investment to add to an already proven position.

BEAR   An investor who believes the market will fall.

BLUE CHIP   Active, well-known, high-quality investment.

BOARD LOT   Regular trading unit which has uniformly been decided upon by the stock exchanges.

BOND   A certificate which is evidence of a debt on which the issue promises to pay interest.

BULL   An investor who believes the market will rise.

CALL OPTION   An option giving the buyer the right to purchase a specified amount, usually 100 shares, of the underlying security at a fixed price and within a specified time period. (Conversely, the seller of a call undertakes an obligation to sell the underlying security at a fixed price within the specified time period should the call buyer decide to exercise the call.)

CALLABLE   A security that may be redeemed by the issuer.

CAPITAL GAIN OR LOSS   Profit or loss resulting from the sale of a capital asset.

CASH FLOW   A company's net income plus any deductions not paid out in actual cash.

CLOSING TRANSACTION   A transaction in which an investor who has written an option terminates his or her position by purchasing an option having the same terms as the initial option.

COMMON STOCK   Securities which represent ownership in a corporation and usually carry voting privileges.

COVERED WRITER   A writer of a call option who owns the underlying security covered by the same number of options.

CONVERTIBLE   A security which may be exchanged by the owner, usually for the common stock of the same company.

CURRENT YIELD   The annual income from an investment expressed as a percentage of the investment's current value.

DEBENTURE   A certificate of indebtedness of a government or company.

DEFAULT   A bond is in default when the borrower cannot live up to the obligation to pay interest or has failed to redeem the bonds at maturity.

DISCOUNT   The amount by which a bond or debenture sells below its par value (usually 100).

DIVIDEND   An amount distributed out of a company's profits to its shareholders.

DOLLAR COST AVERAGING A theory of investing a fixed amount in a security at regular time intervals, thereby averaging the cost paid per unit.

EXERCISE NOTICE   The holder of an option advising the writer that the holder intends to exercise the option.

EXERCISE PRICE   The fixed price at which the underlying security will be bought or sold at the time of exercise.

EXPIRATION DATE   The last day on which the option buyer may exercise the option.

FACE VALUE   The value of a bond that appears on the face of the certificate.

IN-THE-MONEY CALL OPTION   The stock price is higher than the exercise of the option.

INTEREST   Money a borrower pays a lender for the use of money. A bond pays interest.

INTRINSIC VALUE   The amount by which an option is in-the-money.

LEVERAGE   The effect of fixed charges such as debt interest on the earnings of a company. Increases or decreases in borrowing magnifies the percentage of increases or decreases in earnings or profits.

LIQUIDITY   The ability of the market in a particular security to absorb a reasonable amount of buying or selling.

LONG   Signifies ownership of a security.

MARGIN The amount paid by the customer when he or she uses credit to purchase securities.

MARGIN SELLING The forced liquidation of an investor's portfolio for failure to maintain an adequate cash balance.

MATURITY The date on which a bond or debenture comes due and is to be paid.

MUTUAL FUND A company that uses its capital to invest in other companies. Mutual funds provide money management for investors.

OPENING TRANSACTION A transaction in which an investor becomes the writer of an option.

OPTION A contract giving the owner the right to buy (call option) or sell (put option) 100 units of the underlying interest at a fixed price during a specified time period.

OUT-OF-THE-MONEY CALL OPTION The stock price is lower than the exercise price.

PAR VALUE The stated face value of a bond or stock as assigned by the company that issued the security.

PREMIUM The cash amount paid by the buyer to the writer/seller for the privilege of owning the option.

PRICE/EARNINGS RATIO A common stock's current market price divided by annual per share earnings.

PUT OPTION A contract that gives the purchaser the right to sell a security at a fixed price within a specified time period. (Conversely, the seller of a put has an obligation to purchase the security at the fixed price within the specified time period should the put holder decide to effect the sale.)

RETRACTABLE BOND A bond issued with a specific maturity date but granting the holder the right to redeem the bond at an earlier date.

ROLLING A POSITION Substituting an option with a different expiration month or exercise price for a previous option position.

STRIKE PRICE The fixed price at which the underlying security will be bought or sold at the time of exercise. (Same as Exercise Price.)

UNCOVERED (NAKED) WRITER A writer not owning the underlying security of an option position.

UNDER MARGIN The failure of an investor to maintain sufficient cash in his or her account.

UNDERLYING SECURITY The stock or bond against which options are bought or sold.

WRITER The seller of an option contract.

YIELD Return on an investment calculated by dividing the money received by the money invested.